THE SECOND DEATH OF
GEORGE MALLORY

THE ENIGMA AND SPIRIT OF MOUNT EVEREST

THE SECOND DEATH OF GEORGE MALLORY

REINHOLD MESSNER

Translated by Tim Carruthers

St. Martin's Press
New York

www.stmartins.com

Design by Michelle McMillian

Title-page image © Corbis

Excerpts from the writings of George L. Mallory and Noel E. Odell are
taken from sources listed in the Notes on Sources and the Bibliography.

The photograph on page 128 is courtesy of Edmund Hillary/Royal Geographical Society. All other photographs and maps are from Reinhold
Messner's archives. Messner thanks Sergio Martini and Liz Hawley for
permission to use some of their material.

Library of Congress Cataloging-in-Publication Data
Messner, Reinhold.
   [Mallorys zweiter Tod. English]
   The second death of George Mallory : the enigma and spirit of
Mount Everest / Reinhold Messner ; translated from the German by
Tim Carruthers.
      p. cm.
   ISBN 0-312-26806-8
   1. Mountaineering—Everest, Mount (China and Nepal) 2. Mount
Everest Expedition (1924) 3. Leigh-Mallory, George Herbert,
1886–1924. 4. Mountaineers—Great Britain—Biography. I. Title.

GV199.44.E85 M4813 2001
796.52'2'092—dc21
[B]   00-045996

First published in Germany by BLV Verlagsgesellschaft mbH under the
title *Mallory's Zweiter Tod: Das Everest-Rätsel und die Antwort.*

First U.S. Edition: April 2001

10   9   8   7   6   5   4   3   2   1

For Gesar Simon,
who also wants to take the lead

CONTENTS

The north side of Everest, 1924

1. Camp VI at 8,140 meters
2. Somervell's 1924 high-point
3. Norton's 1924 high-point
4. The Second Step: last sighting of Mallory and Irvine
5. First Step
6. The point reached by Finch and Geoffrey Bruce in 1922
7. The point reached by Mallory, Norton, and Somervell in 1922
8. The summit of Mount Everest at 8,848 meters

Of the two alternatives, to turn back a third time, or to die, the latter was for Mallory probably the easier. The agony of the first would be more than he as a man, as a mountaineer, and as an artist, could endure.

—SIR FRANCIS YOUNGHUSBAND,
PRESIDENT OF THE ROYAL
GEOGRAPHICAL SOCIETY, 1926

It has always been my pet plan to climb the mountain gasless with two camps above the Chang La. The gasless party has the better adventure. . . . Still, the conquest of the mountain is the great thing. . . . The whole plan is mine and will give me, perhaps, the best chance of all of getting to the top. It is almost unthinkable with this plan that *I* shan't get to the top; I can't see myself coming down defeated. My intention is to carry as little as possible, move fast and catch the summit by surprise.

—GEORGE LEIGH MALLORY, 1924

THE SECOND DEATH OF
GEORGE MALLORY

CHAPTER ONE

THE MAN, THE MOUNTAIN, THE MYTH

George L. Mallory as a young man

I can well picture Mallory, even in that thin air that barely keeps the fires of energy aglow, responding to the challenge of the Second Step. Were there ever so many voices urging a man to accept that challenge? This is the last chance of carrying out what you came these thousands of miles to do. Once above this step, the way is open to the final pyramid. Few places are more likely to drive a man to the extreme limit of what he can climb than a difficult step upon what is regarded as an easy mountain. Mallory's balance was so good that he was accustomed to move on slabs, where the slightest mistake would mean a fall, as if they were on level ground; he seemed to have no consciousness of how small the safety margin was.

—R. L. G. IRVINE

The summit of Mount Everest seen from the north

FIFTY YEARS AGO, when I was a young boy, my mother read to me about George L. Mallory and Andrew Irvine. I can never forget the first time I heard their story—by the light of a petroleum lamp in a mountain hut in the Dolomites. Since then, they have fueled my reveries and haunted my dreams. "Perfect weather for the job," Mallory had scribbled on a scrap of paper at the last camp on the afternoon of June 7, 1924. The following morning, he and his twenty-two-year-old partner shouldered their heavy oxygen sets and trudged up the steep scree slopes from Camp VI, heading for the rock steps—and the summit of Mount Everest. They never returned.

Mallory's last climb remains a masterpiece in the annals of high-altitude mountaineering. Whether or not it took him to Everest's summit, it remains the most significant ascent ever made on Mount Everest. It is a story that merits retelling: how a man, a schoolteacher by profession, clad in a tweed jacket, makeshift gaiters wrapped around his legs and hobnailed boots on his feet, and with a head full of Romantic ideals, set out to conquer that bastion of rock that was considered un-conquerable.

A survey conducted by James Nicholson in 1849 had es-tablished Mount Everest, then known as Peak XV, as the highest mountain on earth. The task was by no means easy, since the survey instrument weighed half a ton and had first to be transported by twelve people across the pathless terrain of the Himalayan foothills and then calibrated before mea-surements could be taken. After Nicholson had completed his measurements, seven years passed before the business of cal-culation and evaluation was complete and Andrew Waugh—who had taken over from George Everest as surveyor general of the British India Survey—was able to enter a summit height of 29,002 feet (8,840 meters) on the map. In 1856 the Royal Geographic Society bestowed the name Mount Ever-est on the peak in honor of Sir George Everest. Only rarely is the ancient Tibetan name Chomolunga or Chomolungma, meaning "goddess mother of the earth," used. The accuracy of the 1849 calculations is astonishing. In September 1992, surveyors using state-of-the-art GPS equipment determined the exact height of Mount Everest to be 8,848 meters, a dif-ference of roughly twenty feet.

After the turn of the twentieth century, Mount Everest was much more than simply the highest mountain on earth. The English, in particular, saw this icy peak as the last great op-portunity. Having arrived too late at the north and south poles, they set out for the Himalayas in the 1920s. Equipped

Sir George Everest

with tents, ice axes, and hemp ropes, they doggedly pursued their lofty goal, approaching it from the north, the Tibet side, and tackling prejudice, cold, and hopelessness on the way.

An initial reconnaissance expedition, with Mallory as lead climber, got as far as the North Col in 1921. In 1922, Mallory returned to his mountain, this time with steel oxygen bottles in his luggage and a column of porters in his wake—a half dozen of whom were to die in an avalanche. Together with Edward Norton and Howard Somervell, he pushed the route to an unprecedented altitude of well over 8,000 meters. Finally in 1924, Mallory and Irvine made their final ascent.

Their disappearance in the "death zone" rapidly achieved legendary status. For seven and a half decades, geographers, tourists, mountain guides, Sherpas, and most of all mountaineering historians have speculated about whether Mallory attained his goal. Officially, of course, New Zealander Edmund Hillary and Tensing Norgay first successfully climbed Mount Everest on May 29, 1953, from the southern, Nepalese, side. Their photos, not those of Mallory and Irvine, adorn the history books. Hillary and Tensing returned from the Roof of

Andrew Irvine

the World to the stone huts in the valleys of the poor kingdom of Nepal in time for the celebrations to mark the coronation of Queen Elizabeth II. They became heroes; Mallory and Irvine remained ghosts.

Over the years, Mallory's disappearance has inspired intense speculation and plentiful rumors. In 1933 an ice ax, undoubtedly belonging to either Irvine or Mallory, was found at over 8,400 meters. In 1960, Chinese climbers reported finding the remains of a rope and some wooden wedges above the steep rock pitch of the Second Step. Shortly before he died, one of the Chinese maintained that he had happened across a dead body with tattered clothing at about 8,300 meters. This report was not taken seriously. A number of climbers have hallucinated meeting the dead man.

In May 1999, a search party led by American climber Eric Simonson followed Mallory's ascent. Near the spot where the ice ax had been found in 1933, another American, Conrad Anker, saw something out of the ordinary—on a rock ledge at 8,250 meters. What looked like a "strange patch of white" was soon identified as the body of George L. Mallory.

Although remarkably well preserved, Mallory's corpse gave no clue as to the manner of death. Did Mallory die of hypothermia, suffocation, or as a result of injuries? Mallory's snow goggles were in his pocket, suggesting that something had happened as darkness fell. Or during a whiteout. Or even while he was in the throes of delirium. Nor does the location of the body prove or disprove that Mallory and Irvine climbed the Second Step. When death found them, they might have turned back and been attempting to descend directly to their camp. Or they might have reached the summit and died on the way down. Finding their camera, with photographs taken from the highest point on earth, would provide proof positive. To this day, of course, the camera remains lost.

Mallory's disappearance on Mount Everest was never the only tragedy as far as I was concerned. I have long mourned what I call his "second death"—the disappearance of the spirit of amateurism that drove him. Today's modern speed climber is well prepared and pre-equipped. In 1975, Chinese climbers carted long aluminum ladders up to the Second Step, attached them to the steep rock wall, and gave themselves a "bunk up." Pitons were hammered into the rock, the ladders fixed in place, ropes tensioned off. All subsequent Everest expeditions have used these artificial climbing aids, replacing when necessary rotten ropes with new ones. Although the Second Step has in the meantime been "free"-climbed by Conrad Anker—with fixed ropes and ladders within easy reach—no one has yet mastered this obstacle by what I consider "fair means." Mallory had climbed into the unknown, outfitted only with his nailed boots and determination. No one would today attempt the ascent with the kind of equipment Mallory used. He approached Everest on his terms, hoping, as he said, to "catch the summit by surprise." He did not attempt to climb Everest to set a record or make headlines. He did it simply "because it is there."

Since 1980, when I solo-climbed Mount Everest, I have harbored the suspicion that Mallory and Irvine did not reach the summit. I am also convinced that they risked everything to get there. Their pioneering deed overshadows all subsequent mountaineering achievements, my own included. I felt Mallory's presence during my solo ascent of the north-face route. Sometimes, when looking at photographs from his era, I can hear his voice. I know of course that it is my own. Yet I believe that only by trying to see events through Mallory's eyes can we truly rediscover him. Therefore in these pages I will not only quote from Mallory's journals and writings, but imagine what he would have thought about those who followed in his footsteps—whether they have sought merely to climb Everest or, like him, to capture its spirit.

CHAPTER TWO

1921: HEADING EAST

The members of the 1921 expedition. Standing (from the left): Wollaston, Howard-Bury, Heron, and Raeburn. Seated (from the left): Mallory, Wheeler, Bullock, and Morshead

Fate cannot impress me. I have always avoided such in-
dolent things. Even symbols hold no fears for me. I simply
enjoy traveling onwards in such an uncertain direction.
Up and away, to the Himalayas. Maybe it is your direction too, good sir. It is certainly my goal.

—ARNOLT BRONNEN

The mission of the 1921 Reconnaissance had been ful-
filled, every doubt removed. The Spur which rises from
the North Col to the Shoulder of Everest's South-East
Ridge was nothing but easy slabs and moderate snow-
slopes. The expedition could withdraw with a clear
conscience.

—GÜNTER OSKAR DYHRENFURTH

THE NORTH AND SOUTH poles had both been reached. All that now remained was the "east pole," around which British mountaineering was henceforth to revolve. For four years that is what occupied Mallory too. It was as if Mount Everest remained the only goal left, and his small world focused on it, and on it alone. In 1921 he could not yet imagine that this mountain had only one summit, one attraction, and one price. Its true value lay in the secret of its being as yet unclimbed.

Mount Everest had already been recognized as the highest mountain in the world and its summit height had already been accurately surveyed when, in 1904, after a gruesome military action, Sir Francis Younghusband succeeded in securing permission from the Dalai Lama in Lhasa for British mountaineers to climb in the Tibetan part of the Himalaya. But it was only in 1921 that they were ready to mount a reconnaissance expedition.

5.18.1921

When we started our travels in 1921, it was a trian-
gulated peak with a position on the map; but from
the mountaineer's point of view almost nothing was
known. Mount Everest had been seen and photographed from various points on the Singalila ridge
as well as from Kampa Dzong; from these photographs it may be dimly made out that snow lies on
the upper part of the Eastern face at no very steep angle, while the arête bounding this face on the North
comes down gently for a considerable distance. . . .
The North-west sides of the mountain had never
been photographed and nothing was known of its
lower parts anywhere. Perhaps the distant view most
valuable to a mountaineer is that from Sandakphu,
because it suggests gigantic precipices on the South
side of the mountain so that he need have no regrets
that access is barred in that direction for political rea-
sons.

The reconnaissance begins in Khamba Dzong, when they
are still seventy-five miles from the mountain. From the start,
the expedition is plagued by a series of misfortunes. The most
tragic is the sudden death in Khamba Dzong of the expedition doctor, Dr. Kellas, from a heart attack. As a result, only
Bullock and Mallory remain as the sole representatives of the
Alpine Club and the reconnaissance team. Mallory is moved
to write:

It may seem an irony of fate that actually on the day after the distressing event of Dr. Kellas' death we experienced the strange elation of seeing Everest for the first time. It was a perfect early morning as we plodded up the barren slopes above our camp and rising behind the old rugged fort which is itself a singularly impressive and dramatic spectacle; we had mounted perhaps a thousand feet when we stayed and turned, and saw what we came to see. There was no mistaking the two great peaks in the West: that to the left must be Makalu, grey, severe and yet distinctly graceful, and the other away to the right—who could doubt its identity? It was a prodigious white fang excrescent from the jaw of the world. We saw Mount Everest not quite sharply defined on account of a slight haze in that direction; this circumstance added a touch of mystery and grandeur; we were satisfied that the highest of mountains would not disappoint us.

Heading west from Khamba Dzong, they lose sight of Mount Everest as the tip of the summit disappears behind the Gyanka Mountains.

6.11.1921

From Gyanka Nangpa, which lies under a rocky summit over 20,000 feet high, Bullock and I, on June 11, made an early start and proceeded down the gorge. It was a perfect morning and for once we had

15

tolerably swift animals to ride; we were fortunate in choosing the right place to ford the river and our spirits were high. How could they be otherwise? Ever since we had lost sight of Everest the Gyanka Mountains had been our ultimate horizon to the West. Day by day as we had approached them our thoughts had concentrated more and more upon what lay beyond. On the far side was a new country.

For Mallory, his first sight of Mount Everest is a defining moment. From now on his life acquires a new direction. Mallory frequently reflects in his journals on the effect the mountain has on him.

> *It is possible that even Bullock quaked at this sight; everyone did in his own way. I just a little more. For it depended entirely on me as to whether the myth of the mountain was to be transformed and the path found between the supernatural and reality. It was in me that all expectations were vested.*

We were now able to make out almost exactly where Everest should be; but the clouds were dark in that direction. We gazed at them intently through field glasses as though by some miracle we might pierce the veil. Presently the miracle happened. We caught the gleam of snow behind the grey mists. A whole group of mountains began to appear in gigantic fragments. Mountain shapes are often fantastic seen

Mount Everest from the east

through a mist; these were like the wildest creation of a dream. A preposterous triangular lump rose out of the depths; its edge came leaping up at an angle of about 70 degrees and ended nowhere. To the left a black serrated crest was hanging in the sky incredibly. Gradually, very gradually, we saw the great mountain sides and glaciers and arêtes, now one fragment and now another through the floating rifts, until far higher in the sky than imagination had dared to suggest the white summit of Everest appeared.

6.23.1921

Looking at the mountain from a northeasterly direction, they can make out a long ridge running down toward them. Not far below the summit the ridge forms a black shoulder, which Mallory believes is unclimbable. To the right, a section of the ridge is visible in profile against the sky, and this part at least is not unduly steep.

> The task before us was not likely to prove a simple and straightforward matter, and we had no expectation that it would be quickly concluded. It would be necessary in the first place to find the mountain. . . . And there would be more than one approach to be found. We should have to explore a number of valleys radiating from Everest and separated by high ridges which would make lateral communication extremely difficult; we must learn from which direction various parts of the mountain could most conveniently be reached.

And beyond all investigation of the approaches we should have to scrutinize Mount Everest itself. Our reconnaissance must aim at a complete knowledge of the various faces and arêtes, a correct understanding of the whole form and structure of the mountain.

I was fully aware of the size of the task I had set myself. My opponent was a giant! Where was his Achilles' heel, the chink in the armor? Where could I find a glimmer of hope? For only there did I wish to risk my luck. The summit assault was another matter, a matter for me alone.

It turns out that Mount Everest is not all that hard to find:

[W]e chose the Northern approach. We learned from local knowledge that in two days we might reach a village and monastery called Chöbuk, and from there could follow a long valley to Everest. And so it proved. Chöbuk was not reached without some difficulty, but this was occasioned not by obstacles in the country but by the manners of the Tibetans. In Tingri we had hired four pack animals. We had proceeded 2 or 3 miles across the plain when we perceived they were heading in the wrong direction. We were trusting to the guidance of their local drivers and felt very uncertain as to where exactly we should be aiming; but their line was about 60 degrees to the South of our objective according to a guesswork compass bearing. An almost interminable three-cornered argument followed. It appeared that our guides intended to take five days to Chöbuk. They knew all about "ca' canny." In the end we decided to take the risk of a separation; Gyalzen went with the bullocks and our tents to change transport at the village where we were intended to stay the night, while the rest of us made a bee line for a bridge where we should have to cross the Rongbuk stream. At the foot of a vast moraine we waited on the edge of the "maidan," anxiously hoping that we should see some sign of fresh animals approaching; and at length we saw them. It was a late camp that evening on a strip of meadow beside the stream, but we had the comfort of reflecting that we had foiled the natives, whose aim was to retard our progress, and in the sequel we reached our destination with no further trouble.

6.25.1921

They ford the river at Chöbuk, driving the animals loaded with provisions through the water, and follow the right-hand bank of the Rongbuk toward the glacier.

About an hour above Chöbuk they enter a gorge with red walls soaring up on their left. Below them a strip of fertile ground is covered with grass, low bushes, rhododendron, juniper, and yellow aster. Gradually, the path narrows between two chortens:

We paused here in sheer astonishment. Perhaps we had half expected to see Mount Everest at this moment. In the back of my mind were a host of questions clamouring for answers. But the sight of it now banished every thought. We asked no questions and made no comment, but simply looked.

It is perhaps because Everest presented itself so dramatically on this occasion that I find the Northern aspect more particularly imagined in my mind, when I recall the mountain. But in any case this aspect has a special significance. The Rongbuk Valley is well constructed to show off the peak at its head; for about 20 miles it is extraordinarily straight and in that distance rises only 4,000 feet. . . . At the end of the valley and above the glacier Everest rises not so much as a peak as a prodigious mountain mass. . . . There is no complication for the eye. We do not see jagged crests and a multitude of pinnacles. . . . The outline is comparatively smooth because the stratification is horizontal.

And yet Everest is a rugged giant. It has not the smooth undulations of a snow mountain with white snow cap and glaciated flanks. It is rather a great rock mass, coated often with a thin layer of white powder which is blown about its sides. . . . One such place is the long arm of the North-west arête which with its slightly articulated buttresses is like the nave of a vast cathedral roofed with snow. I was, in fact, reminded often by this Northern view of Winchester Cathedral with its long high nave and low square tower; it is only at a considerable distance that one appreciates the great height of this building and the strength which seems capable of supporting a far taller tower. Similarly with Everest; the summit lies back so far along the immense arêtes that big as it always appears one required a distant view to realise its height; and it has no spire though it might easily bear one; I have thought sometimes that a Matterhorn might be piled on the top of Everest and the gigantic structure would support the added weight in stable equanimity.

6.26.1921

After a three-day journey from their headquarters in Tingri, Mallory and Bullock establish camp in full view of Mount Everest. This spot in the Rongbuk Valley will serve as their camp for four weeks.

Back then I was able to wait and content to wait; for the right moment, for my destiny, for the chance of a lifetime. For it was up to me, and me alone, whether or not Mount Everest was climbed. A kind of relationship had developed between the mountain and me, which had to grow and endure in order to become timeless, even after my death.

Neither Bullock nor Mallory has any experience climbing mountains other than those in the Alps. They use their Alpine experience to acquaint themselves with the topography of the mountains and to estimate the time and energy required to scale a certain stretch. However, they quickly realize that their Alpine experience has not fully prepared them for this climb. In the Alps the major glaciers offer direct routes to the peaks. The terrain is much different in Tibet. Steep ledges, loose rocks, and impassable steps make a direct approach impossible. Progress is slow.

> *I was not as good a rock climber as many people might have wished and perhaps Longstaff was right to say that my reputation as a mountaineer was founded less on my successful routes than on all those mountains on which I had failed.*

The climbers must also help the porters adjust. Although they are at home in the mountains, they are not mountaineers. They have to learn the art of moving safely over snow and ice, climbing easy rock pitches, and using ropes and ice axes. Each little reconnaissance trip brings them all a little further on.

6.27.1921

Mallory and Bullock prepare for a long and difficult scouting mission, but nothing prepares them for the intense disappointment of failure:

> No course seemed to lead anywhere. When would our troubles be at an end? In the Alps it has often seemed laborious to go up hill towards the end of a day: it was a new sensation to find it an almost impossible exertion to drag oneself up a matter of 150 feet. . . . I seemed to notice some enervating influence which had not affected me elsewhere. It was the glacier that had knocked me out, not the hard work

23

alone but some malignant quality in the atmosphere, which I can neither describe nor explain.

The lack of oxygen is beginning to affect both climbers.

6.28.1921

Mallory decides to spend a lazy day in camp.

The mountain appears not to be intended for climbing. I've no inclination to think about it in steps to the summit. Nevertheless, we gaze much through fieldglasses. E. is, generally speaking, convex, steep in lower parts and slanting back to the summit. Last section of [North]-east arête should go.

The people back home on their barstools should really take a look at these precipices for themselves! Mountains are not the same in photographs. All these pictures are nothing but a world of lies, of self-deception. With our inner eye we all see blinded men with ice axes crawling up a snow slope when we think of the summit of Everest. This rocky bastion of a mountain is not for mountaineers strolling along half-asleep. Indeed there was more in store for us than I with all my rose-tinted optimism could ever imagine.

6.29.1921

An exciting day with destination unfixed . . . and it's much better to be further on. Real good luck. . . . Meanwhile the idea was growing, the vision of Ever-

est as a structural whole. . . . This idea resembled the
beginning of an artist's painting, a mere rough design
at the start, but growing by steps of clearer definition
in one part and another towards the precise comple-
tion of a whole.

Instead of answering questions, each new expedition only
raises more. Mallory is overwhelmed with new impressions.

7.1.1921
The tired company slowly makes its way up the glacier.

On July 1 I set out with five coolies to reach the head
of the great cwm under the North face of Mount
Everest. The snow on the upper glacier was soft and
made very heavy going. Bad weather came up and in
a race against the clouds we were beaten and failed to
find out what happened to the glacier at its Western
head under the North-west arête. I was now sure that
before attempting to reach this [North] col from the
Rongbuk Glacier, if ever we determined to reach it,
we should have to reconnoitre the other side and if
possible find a more hopeful alternative.

*How matter of fact we mountaineers are about deceiving our-
selves. I only need to read my report from 1921. What use
are all the beautiful descriptions? You just have to imagine
it: damp socks in the tent, sickness-inducing petroleum
fumes, greasy hands, all the mess. Inability to act due to lack*

of practice is the main reason for the dilemma. but even when we recognize the causes it does not hold us back. The self-deception continues, as a small measure of consolation after every route. The first rule of the mountaineer, that he should seek comfort as long as it is possible to do so, should be replaced by the challenge that it would be eminently more sensible to stay at home.

7.12.1921

Mallory and Bullock set out to reconnoiter the Lho La and the south side of Mount Everest.

[W]e halted at 8 A.M. in a thick mist with a nasty wind and some snow falling. And as we went on with the high wind blowing the snow into our faces so that nothing could clearly be distinguished we had the sense of a narrowing place and a perception of the even surface being broken up into large crevasses on one side and the other. At 9:30 we could go no further. Coming out on to a little spur we stood peering down through the mist and knew ourselves to be on the edge of a considerable precipice.

Not a single feature of the landscape around us was even faintly visible in the cloud. For a time we stayed on with the dim hope of better things and then reluctantly retired, baffled and bewildered.

Where had we been? It was impossible to know; but at least it was certain there was no clear way to the

West side of Everest. We could only suppose that we had reached a col on the frontier of Nepal.

A further disappointment awaited us when we reached camp at 1 P.M. I had made a simple plan to ensure our supply of high-protein energy bars and rations from the base camp. The supplies had not come up . . .

Since there is no firewood in the Rongbuk Valley, they are dependent on deliveries of dung from Chöbuk. The uncharitable weather means they keenly miss the comfort and warmth of an open fire.

7.19.1921

Mallory and Bullock set off while it is yet dark and fairly cloudy. The moon peeps over the ridges and casts crazy shadows onto the snow. The coal-black outline of a monstrous tooth stares back at them in the pale light. As the moon sets, it becomes light enough to dispense with the lanterns. As day breaks, the sky is still overcast but the clouds are dispersing like guilty souls. At six o'clock they look down into the Western Cwm from the col of the Lho La; the first rays of sun hit the Western Summit. The Khumbu Valley, awesome and terrifying in the frosty light of morning, remains in the shadow of Mount Everest.

But another disappointment—it is a big drop about 1,500 feet down to the glacier, and a hopeless precipice. I was hoping to get away to the left and traverse into the cwm; that too quite hopeless. However, we have seen this Western glacier and are not sorry we have not to go up it. It is terribly steep and broken. In any case work on this side could only be carried out from a base in Nepal, so we have done with the Western side. It was not a very likely chance that the gap between Everest and the South Peak [Lhotse] could be reached from the West. It is a big world! . . . We still had to see other parts of the mountain. . . . Could the North col be reached from the East and how could we attain this point?

Do I have to admit that I was the one to let slip the key to Mount Everest? No, in those days the Khumbu Icefall really was impossible and even later generations of mountaineers would have risked an ascent from the north had they been able to do so. All in all, the approach to the mountain from Tibet is easier.

7.25.1921

The reconnaissance party returns to camp to find a letter has arrived from Colonel Howard-Bury informing them that he is setting off from Tingri on July 23 for Kharta and will be spending the night in Chöbuk two days later.

The side valley of Kharta has long been the object of Mallory and Bullock's curiosity, so they decide to set off now through uncharted territory to get there. They calculate that food for eight days should be sufficient. Howard–Bury would arrive soon enough with the bulk of the supplies anyway. But things went wrong from the beginning:

> [It] transpired that our organisation was not running smoothly—it never did run smoothly so long as we employed, as an indispensable Sirdar, a whey-faced treacherous knave whose sly and calculated villainy too often, before it was discovered, deprived our coolies of their food, and whose aquiescence in his own illimitable incompetence was only less disgusting than his infamous duplicity. It was the hopeless sense that things were bound to go wrong if we trusted this man's services—and we had no one else at that time through whom it was possible to order supplies from the natives—that turned the scale and spoilt the plan.

> *The question of why we at first paid no attention to the Rongbuk Glacier and later completely forgot about it is embarrassing. I was too busy thinking about the summit. The East Ronguk Glacier is, however, the best approach to the North Col and anyone who sees the glacier will say that this is the natural route to the summit of Everest. Coming from the east I had seen the Rongbuk Glacier and noticed its deep snow basin toward the south. If however the basin was so important how could the stream be so unimportant? I asked myself. But perhaps mountaineering, just like love, is blind. Even if the outflow of the East Rongbuk Glacier is remark-*

able because of its astonishingly low water level, obsessive mountaineers are apparently quite simply sadly lacking in imagination.

The journey to Kharta is uneventful. The base camp established by Colonel Howard-Bury in Kharta proves to be ideal. Here they rest their tired bodies after the hardships in the high mountains. Kharta lies at a relatively low altitude and the climate is pleasant. The air is mild and without the oppressive heat; the sun shines brightly, without burning; the clouds dispense gentle showers, without ever turning into constant rain. And since the village lies on the main trade route to Nepal, fresh produce is always available.

But perhaps after life in the Rongbuk Valley, with hardly a green thing to look at and too much of the endless unfriendly stone-shoots and the ugly waste of glaciers, and even after visions of sublime snow-beauty, a change was more needed for the mind. It was a delight to be again in a land of flowery meadows and trees and crops; to look into the deep green gorge only a mile away where the Arun goes down into Nepal was to be reminded of a rich vegetation and teeming life, a contrast full of pleasure with Nature's niggardliness in arid, wind-swept Tibet.

The Kharta base, besides, was convenient for our reconnaissance. Below us a broad glacier stream joined the Arun above the gorge; it was the first met with since we had left the Rongbuk stream; it came down from the West and therefore, presumably, from Everest. To follow it up was an obvious plan as the next stage of our activities. After four clear days of idleness and reorganization at Kharta we set forth again on August 2 with this object.

8.2.1921

Mallory and Bullock ask the village leaders to find guides with knowledge of the area to accompany the expedition to Chomolungma. These experienced local men will show them the best places to cross the stream and prevent them from taking any wrong turns at the many forks in the valley.

The porters are listless. Bullock and Mallory decide to lead the caravan of porters from the rear to monitor the expedition's progress. The valley is so well endowed with hamlets and farmsteads, ideal for unauthorized breaks, that the leaders fear they will lose half of the men and equipment.

It was a slow march this day; we had barely accomplished 8 miles when Bullock and I with the hindmost came round a shoulder on the right bank about 4 P.M. and found the tents pitched on a grassy shelf and looking up a valley where a stream came in from our left. The Tibetan herdsman and his Tibetan coolies who were carrying some of our loads had evidently no intention of going further. . . . We were at a valley junction of which we had heard tell, and the headman pointed the way to the left. Here indeed was a valley, but no glacier stream. . . . Where were we going and what should we find? The headman announced that it would take five more days to reach Chomolungma.

I just explained, briefly, that he was to get us up there in two. No arguments—just get on with it! In this way I gained respect. What were these people thinking? How, if not as a giver of orders, was I to train the porters to do my bidding and thus help me achieve my aims? How else could they know what I expected of them?

What they got up to on the first day they put right on the second. They did as I commanded. Only in this way were we able to pass beyond the "rhododendron border" in good time and continue on to Mount Everest, getting ever nearer to the destination of my desires. No reproaches please! What would the porters have had to gain if I had given up? Nothing. So it was for their benefit too, and not just for mine, that I drove them on.

When the reconnaissance group arrives at the Langma La, twelve hundred meters above the last camp, Mallory is faced with something of a mystery. While he waits for the mist to part, he not only finds himself wondering whether the Tibetan porters—who are not as strong as the Sherpas and have to carry the wet tents—will follow, but also where the mountain is.

In the Sahib's tent that night there took place a long and fragmentary conversation with the headman, our Sirdar acting as interpreter. We gained one piece of information: there were two Chomolungmas. It was not difficult to guess that, if Everest were one, the other must be Makalu.

I asked to be guided to the greatest of all Chomolungmas. Had I not always wanted the highest and best both for myself and the others?

8.4.1921

The morning dawns clear. They think it is the perfect weather for more thorough reconnaissance. They descend into the valley, cross the river by a vertiginous bridge, pick their way through dwarf rhododendrons, and wander across pleasant meadows. Reaching a glacier, they follow its left-hand side.

> Towards mid-day the weather showed signs of clearing; suddenly on our left across the glacier we saw gigantic precipices looming through the clouds. But we saw no more. In a few moments the grey clouds blowing swiftly up from below had enveloped us, rain began to fall heavily, and when eventually we came to broad meadows above the glaciers, where yaks were grazing and Tibetan tents were pitched, we were content to stop. There was indeed no point in going farther; we had no desire to run our heads against the East face of Everest; we must now wait for a view.

This attempt thwarted, they decide to return to camp and wait for the weather to clear.

8.5.1921

When Mallory pokes his nose out of the tent, the weather is much improved. The clouds are melting off the mountains and the sun is bright. Looking to his right, Mallory spies a huge ridge. The entire mass of the east flank gradually reveals itself to an astonished Mallory.

This awesome vision of grandeur fills him with wonder. At the broad head of the valley stands the summit pyramid of Everest. Below it a basin of fragmented ice catches the tributaries of the glacier pouring down between the supporting buttresses of Mount Everest. The charm of this beautiful vision has more to do with Mallory's imagination than with geography.

> *One image lives on in my memory as the overwhelming impression: Mount Everest with its South Summit and its enormous southeast shoulder. The highest mountain in the world! Today, the story of the east face of Everest provides plenty of fuel for the imagination. If only I had known all that then. From Ed Webster's insanity to my own despair on the Second Step—I would have gone mad. What is fiction compared with factual reports and such a spectacle?*
>
> *Again and again my eye followed the ascending lines, the mighty shoulders, the ridges and the jagged edge of the hanging glacier that covers the upper part of the east face of Everest. If only we were up there now! I found that the splendor of the high mountain chain was merely increased by such a charming foreground. Only when I had dreamed long*

enough about Chomolungma, the Mother Goddess of the World, and about Cho Oyu, the Turquoise Goddess, did I find my way back to the valley floor, to the green meadows where our tents stood in the wind, where the cattle were grazing and where the delicious buttermilk stood cooling in the stream. Although my spirit had found its home high up there with the gods, I remained loyal to these more gentle beings that gave life to the countryside at their feet.

Mallory turns his attention to a white peak by the name of Carpo-ri, which lies on the watershed. If they could climb it, they would not only be able to look down into the East Rongbuk Valley and across to the Chang La but would have a grand view of the whole of the east flank of Mount Everest.

The deviation from our intended line of approach involved by entering the Kama Valley was not one which we were likely to regret. In so far as our object was to follow up a glacier to the North Col we were now on the wrong side of a watershed. A spur of mountains continues Eastwards from the foot of Everest's North-east arête; these were on our right as we looked up the Kama Valley; the glacier of our quest must lie on the far side of them.

8.6.1921

The reconnaissance team pitches the Whymper tents next to an area of moraine at about 5,300 meters.

Perhaps as night came on and snow was still falling we were vaguely disquieted, but we refused to believe in anything worse than the heavens' passing spite, and before we put out our candles the weather cleared. We went out into the keen air; it was a night of early moons. We were not kept waiting for the supreme effects; the curtain was withdrawn. Rising from the bright mists Mount Everest above us was immanent, vast, incalculable—no fleeting apparition of elusive dream-form: nothing could have been more set and permanent, steadfast like Keats's star, "in lone splendour hung aloft in the night."

Why is the sublime destined to stand alongside the trivial, the everyday? How could I identify with this mountain? Merely because I wanted to climb it, climb up into the night beneath the stars? It is a state of mind almost like being intoxicated, as thoughts tumble from the sky. Fear, hope, brutal reality are extinguished as darkness falls beneath the firmament.

8.7.1921

A feeling of lassitude, heavier than normal, weighs on the frozen camp. The cook is feeling particularly unwell.

The coolies prolonged their minutes of grace after the warning shout, dallied with the thought of meeting the cold air, procrastinated, drew the blankets more closely round them, and—snored.

36

How I was transformed in those days! I, George Leigh Mal-
lory, a shabbily dressed sahib who usually enjoyed the privi-
lege of being the last to crawl out of his down sleeping bag,
had been out and about for days with great enthusiasm even
if not always with wholehearted dedication. I collected my
frozen belongings together, stumbled over smooth moraine
boulders and by sunrise had already slogged high up the
mountain. There I waited for the miracle: Even before the first
light of dawn the outlines of Mount Everest were brought to
life by a faint blue glow. Later pale yellow, then vibrant blue-
gray flowed over my mountain until finally the sun poured
gold over the summit and the shadows slipped away down the
slopes. In anticipation of the approaching grandeur I stood still
in order to experience this miracle over and over again.

Mallory looks long and hard at the east face of Everest. The
upper part appears to be just an easy-angled snow slope, but
his gaze also falls on the lower edge of the hanging glacier.

It required but little further gazing to be convinced—
to know that almost everywhere the rocks below
must be exposed to ice falling from this glacier; that
if, elsewhere, it might be possible to climb up, the
performance would be too arduous, would take too
much time.

It would be far too dangerous. Mallory is a bold man, but
he is not reckless.

Others might have tackled this wall if they had felt the urge. I was certainly not one of them. I was perhaps mad but I was not tired of living.

The reconnaissance expedition is drawing ever closer to its destination. On reaching the watershed there is an air of excitement and anticipation:

> Below us on the far side was a glacier flowing East, and beyond it two important rock peaks, which we at once suspected must be two triangulated points each above 23,000 feet. Was this at last the valley observed so long ago from the hill above Shiling, more than 50 miles away, to point up towards the gap between Changtse and Everest? As yet we could not say. The head of the glacier was out of sight behind the Northern slopes of our mountain. We must ascend further, probably to its summit, to satisfy our curiosity—to see, we hoped, Changtse and its relation to this glacier, and perhaps the Chang La of our quest.

Climbing on wet snow is strenuous. The altitude is also becoming more of a problem.

> No one without experience of the problem could guess how difficult it may be to sit down with snow-shoes strapped to the feet. The remedy of course is to take off the snow-shoes; but the human mountaineer

after exhausting efforts is too lazy for that at an eleva-
tion of 21,000 feet. He prefers not to sit; he chooses
to lie—in the one convenient posture under the circumstances—flat upon his back and with his toes and
snow-shoes turned vertically upwards. . . . An exami-
nation of the various pairs of upturned toes where the
prostrate forms were still grouped grotesquely in the
snow was not encouraging.

*Life is to be enjoyed—why else climb mountains? At a
height of 6,400 meters the mountaineer is far too lazy to do
the obvious and the necessary, even when it concerns the success of the climb.*

Presently, through a hole in the cloud cover, Mallory
catches a glimpse of Changtse, the North Summit of Everest,
and his eye follows the line of the ridge connecting it to Everest itself, beyond the saddle, or North Col. He is burning with
the desire to see the slopes below the North Col, but they remain hidden from view. A short while later the view of the
northeast opens up. A thin veil of mist is transparent enough
to reveal a glimpse of the North Col. Mallory sees it clearly.

As I looked, if any doubts remained at this time as to
that line of attack, they now received the coup de
grâce. Not only was the crest itself seen to be both
sharp and steep . . . but the slopes on either hand appeared in most places an impracticable alternative; and

leading up to the great rock towers of the North-east shoulder, the final section, the point of the cruel sickle, appeared effectively to bar further progress should anyone have been content to spend a week or so on the lower parts. To discern so much required no prolonged study.

Only a bad mountaineer walks the well-trodden paths. And where there is hope there is also a way. Disappointment must never creep in. The working spirit quickly overcomes hopelessness and suffering.

Their intention now is to follow the glacier up from the end of the main Kharta Valley.

Our next plans were made on the descent. With the relaxation of physical effort the feeling of dazed fatigue wears off and a mind duly strung to activity may work well enough.

But time is running out. They are due back in Kharta on the twentieth for a meeting of the entire expedition team.

8.11.1921
The tents are pitched high up in the Kharta Valley, at an altitude of 5,000 meters. The team ignores two subsidiary streams branching off to the side of the valley. The first, which comes down from the north, is too small to be of consequence; the second does not appear to have a source far enough north.

Ahead of us we had seen that the valley forked; we must follow the larger stream and then no doubt we should come soon to the glacier of our quest and be able at last to determine whether it would serve us to approach Chang La.

It seemed certain that the next two days must provide the climax or anticlimax of our whole reconnaissance. The mystery must surely now be penetrated and the most important discovery of all made.

Mallory now takes the lead and remains in front. When shortly thereafter he becomes sick and Bullock continues on toward the East Rongbuk Glacier without him, Mallory is plagued by dark thoughts. A few hours before dark Bullock reaches a possible campsite, from where he can see the snout of a glacier, and in the evening a porter comes running down the steep, sandy slopes back to base to deliver the following note to Mallory:

> I can see up the glacier ahead of me and it ends in another high pass. I shall get to the pass tomorrow morning if I can, and ought to see our glacier over it. But it looks, after all, as though the most unlikely solution is the right one and the glacier goes out into the Rongbuk Valley.

Into the Rongbuk Valley! They had considered this route but never really thought it possible. Now everything is wide open again.

The mystery deepened. I soon decided that we were looking up the glacier where we had looked down on the 7th. The time had come to abandon our project of finding the foot of the glacier in order to follow it up; for we could more easily come to the head of it and if necessary follow it down.

Mallory places all his hopes on this possibility. They will need four days to get to the Lhakpa La. Although Mallory is still far from fit, they decide to press on with the march as quickly as possible.

Never before had our lungs been tested quite so severely.

Regular breathing in the same rhythm as your steps is the secret of high-altitude mountaineering. It is necessary to adjust the climbing tempo to the rhythm of the lungs. It is no good just using the upper part of the lungs to breathe; you must use the diaphragm as well. The cause of sudden fatigue at high altitudes is always due to the lazy working of the lungs.

They cannot decide which route to take to reach the glacier basin between Lhakpa La and Chang La. Maybe they could use the old base camp at the tongue of the Rongbuk Glacier? But now the weather has taken a turn for the worse again and the mountain is far away.

Although we could hardly see a thing through the cloud, I was prepared, so to speak, to bet my bottom dollar that a way could be found, and was resolved that before we turned homewards this year we must get up from the East. . . . The whole plan of campaign had been founded upon the belief that September would be the best month for climbing, and our greatest efforts, some sort of assault upon the mountain, were timed to take place then. We must now proceed upon the assumption that what the wise men prophesied about the matter would come true; and they promised a fine September. About the beginning of the month the monsoon would come to an end; then we should have a succession of bright, clear days to melt the snow and cold, starry nights to freeze it hard. At worst the calm spell would only be broken by a short anger.

The preliminary reconnaissance work has now been completed. Mallory is pleased with the result. Ahead of him lies the crowning adventure, the summit of all his climbing achievements. He pins his hopes on a September assault.

8.20.1921

The expedition regroups in Kharta, and all the members, climbers, and scientists assemble. They discuss the results of the reconnaissance mission and various approaches to the summit:

On August 20 we went down to Kharta for ten days' rest and reorganisation. The party was gathering there for the assault, in which we all were to help to the best of their powers. Col. Howard-Bury and Mr. Wollaston were there; Dr. Heron came in on the following day, and a little later Major Wheeler. A conversation with this officer, who had been working in the Rongbuk Valley since Bullock and I had left it, was naturally of the highest interest, and he now confirmed what his sketch map had suggested: that the glacier on to which we had looked down from Lhakpa La drained into the Rongbuk Valley. But this certain knowledge could have no bearing on our plans; we remained content with the way we had found and troubled our heads no more for the present about the East Rongbuk Glacier.

9.20.1921

One month later Mallory and Morshead set off with fourteen porters on the carry to the Lhakpa La Pass. The leaders stamp out a path for the heavily laden porters. Although hopes of reaching a high point on Mount Everest are slim, Mallory wants to adhere to the original plan until either it succeeds or circumstances force them to alter it. The conditions are ideal, with a solid, crisp snow base.

We walked briskly over it, directly towards Mount Everest, with all the hope such a performance might inspire.

They still must take frequent breaks, however. Soon the party becomes straggly and disorderly and Mallory goes on ahead to set the pace.

At the col, they have their first clear view of the Chang La and below it a mighty wall of firn snow, perhaps three hundred meters high. How are they to climb this wall and reach the North Col?

Wollaston does not consider himself qualified to join the attempt of the North Col. Of the others, only Wheeler has enough mountain experience to accompany Bullock and Mallory.

9.22.1921

Gusting winds from the northwest make the col bitterly cold. Mallory hopes to continue the ascent with a full complement of porters, but in the morning three men, including two of the best, are too ill to continue. As a result, some of the loads are heavier than he would have liked.

> To me the term mountain sickness *does not mean actually being sick but rather it is a condition of weakness that results in an aversion to undertaking any kind of activity. Somewhere up on the heights it hits us all.*

Once emergency rations for the climbers are left at the Lhakpa La Pass, they proceed down onto the snow beneath the North Col and pitch their tents.

> Fierce squalls of wind visited our tents and shook and worried them with the disagreeable threat of tearing

them away from their moorings, and then scurried off, leaving us to wonder at the change and asking what next to expect.

9.25.1921
The ascent to the North Col begins.

It was an hour or so after sunrise when we left camp and half an hour later we were breaking the crust on the first slopes under the wall. We had taken three coolies who were sufficiently fit and competent, and now proceeded to use them for the hardest work. Apart from one brief spell of cutting when we passed the corner of a bergschrund it was a matter of straightforward plugging, firstly slanting up to the right on partially frozen avalanche snow and then left in one long upward traverse to the summit. Only one passage shortly below the col caused either anxiety or trouble; here the snow was lying at a very steep angle and was deep enough to be disagreeable. About 500 steps of very hard work covered all the worst of the traverse.

They reach the col of the Chang La shortly before midday, tired but not completely spent.

I was now finding my best form; I supposed I might be capable of another 2,000 feet.

Below the steep slope leading to the North Col

During the ascent Mallory often climbs the route from the Col to the rocks of the Northeast Ridge in his mind's eye. Possible, if no strong wind is blowing, he thinks. All his doubts have evaporated. If ever they had doubted the viability of climbing this ridge, Mallory now feels certain that Mount Everest will belong to him.

For a long way up those easy rock and snow slopes was neither danger nor difficulty. But at present there was wind. It came in fierce gusts at frequent intervals, blowing up the powdery snow in a suffocating tourbillon. On the col beyond it was blowing a gale. The powdery fresh snow on the great face of Everest was being swept along in unbroken spindrift and the very ridge where our route lay was marked out to receive its unmitigated fury. To see, in fact, was enough; the wind had settled the question; it would have been folly to go on.

This is the day of the big decision. Either they will have to relocate their camp to the pass or retreat. This is just a taste of the coming storms of winter.

We really were incapable of continuing this adventure. What use would it have been to anyone if I had disappeared at the very first attempt? We had to pull back and wait for a second chance.

They descend carefully from the col and make their way back to Kharta to reorganize and travel home.

Although the first expedition did not reach the summit, their trek up the North Col proved it was a viable route. The vague rib leading from the North Col to the Northeast Shoulder is wide enough to offer a choice of lines of ascent. The ridge is not a knife-edge, but a broad, rounded feature devoid of pinnacles and rock steps. Progress would certainly be smooth, and it would be possible to climb a considerable way along it without meeting any serious obstacles.

But Mallory is still uncertain about this approach. On that narrow edge even the smallest obstacle, a little tower, a six-meter-high wall, a steep step, can hold up or even defeat the strongest of parties. Just before the start of the Northeast Ridge the gradient becomes steeper, and the steep sections increase higher up. In addition to these obstacles, Mallory worries that the pinnacles at the final part of the ridge will be impossible to summit. Back at the Alpine Club in London, Mallory relates his concerns.

> Much will depend upon the possibility of escaping from the crest to avoid the obstacles and of regaining it easily. The South-east side (left going up) is terribly steep, and it will almost certainly be out of the question to traverse there. But the sloping snow-covered ledges on the North-west may serve very well; the difficulty about them is their tendency to be horizontal in direction and to diverge from the arête where it slopes upwards. But one way or another I think it should be possible with the help of such ledges to reach the final obstacle.
>
> The summit itself is like the thin end of a wedge thrust up from the mass in which it is embedded. The edge of it, with the highest point at its far end, can only be reached from the North-east by climbing a steep blunt edge of snow.

"So is the ascent of Mount Everest humanly possible?" Mallory asks the room. Certainly it is. But the chances of success depend on factors other than pure mountaineering considerations and abilities. Success depends as much on the ability to adapt to the thin air and on the capacity for suffering on the part of the summit team. What results could be expected from the use of artificial oxygen? Would the blood's red corpuscles multiply to such a degree as to render a human being capable of withstanding the high altitudes over a prolonged time? Would they even be able to find suitable campsites high up on the mountain? Such questions could only be answered by making an attempt, an attempt where the slightest mistake could prove fatal. However well equipped they might be, the task that lay ahead would place huge demands on the climbers and possibly even exceed the boundaries of human strength and stamina.

It might be possible for two men to struggle somehow to the summit, disregarding every other consideration. It would be a different matter to climb the mountain as mountaineers would have it climbed.

It was necessary to wait for a year before trying again. Despite my confidence in myself there are so many variables to consider when climbing. A breakdown in the supply chain, soft snow, or an avalanche can ruin everything. A storm on the ridge would force even the strongest climber back down. Even the tiniest thing—a boot too narrow by a hair's breadth for a foothold to be safely used, for example—could force the whole team to retreat.

Above all, we must have good luck, great mountaineer-

*ing good fortune: a lucky moment in this horrendous world
in order to be victorious or to die.*

Mallory knows exactly what lies in wait for the aspirant
Everest mountaineer. Even the reconnaissance expedition began tragically, as Irvine later recalled:

> Colonel Howard-Bury, its leader, was not a climber,
> and the mountaineering party suffered serious losses
> before the foot of Everest was reached. Dr. Kellas, a
> Scotsman, who had carried out with the coolies
> alone more ascents of peaks over twenty thousand
> feet than any man living, dies of heart-failure after
> suffering for several days from enteritis on the jour-
> ney though Tibet. Mr. Raeburn, one of the best
> known of British guideless climbers, proved too old
> to stand the strain that Tibet puts upon the heart, the
> lungs and the digestive organs. . . . It was right of him
> [Bullock], however, to consider Mallory as the leader
> of the climbing-party and to leave the initiative to
> him; and Mallory was a man who, as Norton says,
> "jumped into the lead" when difficulties arose.
>
> If the climbing of Everest is, as we have been told,
> an important stage in the victory of mind over mat-
> ter, then let every conceivable method be adopted to
> ensure success. Let dynamite be taken to excavate a
> better platform for the tents at the highest camps; let
> the climbers be in sufficient numbers to be always at

hand to help an exhausted man; let pitons be taken, cables fixed, and oxygen dumped at various points. It is by these mechanical inventions that the superstitious terrors of the natives will be destroyed, far more than by any sacrifice of life or health.

CHAPTER THREE

1922: THE ASSAULT FROM THE NORTH

Mallory and Norton climbing the North Ridge in 1922

This performance aroused widespread admiration, and rightly so: for it had outdistanced the previous 24,600 feet record, which the Duke of Abruzzi's 1909 Expedition had established on Bride Peak (Chogolisa) in the Karakorum, by some 2,400 feet. And for the first time the 26,000 feet line had been crossed by a climbing party—moreoever without the assistance of oxygen-apparatus!

—GÜNTER OSKAR DYHRENFURTH

AS SOON AS the members of the 1921 reconnaissance trip return home, preparations begin for the Second Everest Expedition. Because he speaks the local languages and is held in high regard by Gurkhas, Sherpas, Bhotias, and Tibetans, General Charles G. Bruce is chosen as expedition leader. George L. Mallory is also on the team. For him, Mount Everest is a problem that must be solved.

> I will say nothing about justification for this beyond remarking that it glorifies Mount Everest, since this mountain has not yet been climbed. It is true that I did what I could to reach the summit, but now I look back and see all those wonderful preparations, the great array of boxes collected at Phari Dzong and filling up the courtyard of the bungalow, the train of animals and coolies carrying our baggage across Tibet, the thirteen selected Europeans so snugly wrapt

in their woollen waistcoats and Jaeger pants, their ar-
mour of wind-proof materials, their splendid over-
coats, the furred finneskoes or felt-sided boots or
fleece-lined moccasins devised to keep warm their
feet, and the sixty strong porters with them delight-
ing in underwear from England and leathern jerkins
and puttees from Kashmir; and then, unforgettable
scene, the scatter of our stores at the Base Camp, the
innumerable neatly-made wooden boxes concealing
the rows and rows of tins—of Harris' sausages,
Hunter's hams, Heinz's spaghetti, herrings soi-disant
fresh, sardines, sliced bacon, peas, beans, and a whole
forgotten host besides, sauce bottles for the Mess ta-
bles, and the rare bottles more precious than these,
the gay tins of sweet biscuits, Ginger Nuts and Rich
Mixed, and all the carefully chosen delicacies; and besides all these for our sustenance or pleasure, the fuel
supply, uncovered in the centre of the camp, green
and blue two-gallon-cans of paraffin and petrol, and
an impressive heap of yak-dung; and the climbing
equipment—the gay little tents with crimson flies or
yellow, the bundles of soft sleeping-bags, soft as ei-
derdown quilt can be, the ferocious crampons and
other devices, steel pointed and terrible, for boots'
armament, the business-like coils of rope, the little
army of steel cylinders containing oxygen under high
pressure, and, not least, the warlike sets of apparatus
for using the life-giving gas; and lastly, I call to mind
the whole begoggled crowd moving with slow deter-

The members of the 1922 expedition at Base Camp. Front row (left to right): Mallory, Finch, Longstaff, General Bruce, Strutt, Crawford. Back row (left to right): Morshead, Geoffrey Bruce, Noel, Wakefield, Somervell, Morris, Norton

mination over the snow and up the mountain slopes and with such remarkable persistence bearing up the formidable loads.

The higher the peak, the more the pleasure of climbing it recedes into the background and thus it was that I made the decision to spend a few quiet days at Base Camp before doing very much. Hard work is the major cause of mountain sickness.

5.10.1922

Mallory and Howard Somervell set off for Camp I, reaching it just two and a half hours later. A cook brings them tea and cake and asks what they would like for their main meal. It is a good start.

5.11.1922

It is 10 A.M. when the two men set off for Camp II. The camp, besieged by icy winds on three sides, is bitterly cold.

5.12.1922

They follow the true left edge of the glacier toward Camp III. Strewn with moraines and boulders, the route is especially challenging.

The campsite is perched on rocks that have fallen from the steep slopes of the North Summit. Only a shallow gully separates the campsite from the glacier. Despite all its disadvantages it is still the best place to camp beneath the North Col.

With the Sherpas' help, all of the tents are pitched and a kitchen area is built where they can eat their meals out of the wind.

> Perhaps the most important matter was the instruction of Pou, our cook, in the correct use of the Primus stove; with the purpose of giving him confidence a fine fountain of blazing paraffin was arranged and at once extinguished by opening the safety valve; for the conservation of our fuel supply we carefully showed him how the absolute alcohol must be used to warm the burner while paraffin and petrol were to be mixed for combustion. Fortunately, he rose above those disagreeable agitations which attend the roaring or the

failure of Primus stoves, so that after these first explanations we had never again to begrime our hands with paraffin and soot.

In the evening Somervell and Mallory discuss their plans. Neither of them is feeling particularly well. Instead of climbing any higher immediately, they decide to spend a day in camp and search for a route to the North Col the next day. Mallory already has an approach in mind.

5.13.1922

They set off with Mallory's Sherpa, Dasno, carrying one small tent, ropes, and some wooden pegs about eighteen inches long to serve as snow anchors. With the sun on their backs, they make their way up Mallory's proposed route but find a series of impassable crevasses and steep walls of ice blocking the way. With no clear route available, they construct a detour by cutting steps and fixing ropes in place. The upper slope is quite steep but gives them no trouble, even though the snow is in poor condition. The work is a matter of brute strength more than climbing skill, and their tiredness and lassitude increase; the ice climbing and above all the constant need to keep stamping though the snow are strenuous. Beneath the North Col, Mallory and Somervell confront a crevasse too large to jump. Attempting to work their way back down its length, they find a snow bridge to the opposite edge. It is an extremely dangerous crossing due to their weakened state. If one man should slip and fall into the chasm, it would be impossible for the other to pull him out.

One man on his own will always have the advantage of Mount Everest. Should he not reach the top and perish halfway to the summit he will at least be assured of the prospect of immortality; if he makes it, the victory is his alone. But within the confines of an expedition there are other rules to be observed.

The team is the dilemma. Two is too few as one alone is unable to offer any help should something happen to the other. Thus, three men must climb on a rope. However, as one exhausted climber cannot be left alone without protection from a tent, and the third cannot climb on alone, all three would have to turn back if one is unable to continue. Thus a rope of four is the key as two are able to continue if one has to stay behind with an injured party. But if there are four it is far more likely that someone will indeed take ill, and the remaining two are again only one rope.

5.16.1922

A number of porter loads arrive in Camp III and with them Strutt, Morshead, and Norton. Ten porters are available for the load carries to the North Col. Mallory's hopes are high.

Preparation requires exact calculation. The first thing is to make a list—in this case a list of all we should require at Camp IV, with the approximate weights of each article. But not every article would be available to be carried up on the first of two journeys to the

North Col; for instance, we must keep our sleeping bags for use at Camp III until we moved up ourselves. It was necessary, therefore, to mark off certain things to be left for the second journey, and to ascertain that not more than half of the whole was so reserved. . . . However carefully you have gone over in your mind and prepared for every contingency, you may be quite sure you have omitted something, probably some property of the porters regarded by them as necessary to salvation, and at the last moment it will turn up. On this occasion we took good care to carry up more than half of what was shown on our list on the first journey. Another difficulty is the nature of the loads. They cannot be all exactly equal, because they are composed of indivisible objects. A tent cannot be treated like a vulgar fraction. We intended our loads to be from 25 to 30 lb. They were all weighed with spring balance, and the upper limit was only exceeded by a pound or two in two cases, to the best of my remembrance.

5.17.1922

Fifteen men set off for Camp IV: Mallory, Strutt, Morshead, Norton, Somervell, and ten porters. The snow conditions are good, the tracks clearly visible, but their awareness is dulled due to the high altitude. There is only the mindless drudgery, the dazzling sunlight, and the monotony of the uphill slog. There is not even a breeze.

Slowly and silently they make their steady way uphill. Stamping up the final slope, Strutt suddenly bursts out laughing, gasping for breath: "I wish that—the cinema were here. If I look anything like what I feel, I ought to be immortalized for the British public." They all stare at his yellow-ashen face, and Mallory replies, "Well, what in heaven's name do we look like? And what do we do it for anyway?"

5.18.1922

A day of rest. Everyone is exhausted due to the altitude.

> *There is no point in deceiving oneself about the uncomfortable conditions. Yet I believe that apart from the food, the majority of people soon get used to the discomforts of camp life at high altitudes. Anyone who has been able to tear himself away from house, bed, spring mattress, armchairs, chest of drawers, and bookcase misses little. Only the mealtimes get more and more greasy as time goes on, however well they may have been prepared. We eat like birds of prey. This condition has less to do with the mountaineers returning to their Stone Age roots or with the wholesome abandonment of good table manners by normally civilized people; it can only be blamed upon lack of appetite and the lack of a table, plates, and washing facilities.*

Whenever one of them is hungry, he eats whatever can be prepared most quickly and easily. The basic fare is whatever food they have most of, washed down with as much tea as they can stand before the unpleasant taste of melted snow becomes unbearable.

The Primus stoves remained at Camp III, partly because they were heavy and partly because, however carefully devised, their performance at high altitude must always be a little uncertain. They had served us well up to 21,000 feet, and we had no need to trust them further. With our aluminum cooking sets we could use either absolute alcohol in the spirit burner or "Meta," a French sort of solidified spirit, especially prepared in cylindrical shape and extremely efficient; you have only to put a match to the dry white cylinders and they burn without any trouble, and smokelessly, even at 23,000 feet, for not less than forty minutes. The supply of "Meta" was not very large . . . the alcohol was to do most of our heating at Camp IV.

Why did General Bruce not keep a herd of yaks at base camp to provide us with fresh milk? Merely because there was no grass there or because no one was prepared to share his tent with a yak? So we were stuck with cocoa made from dried milk and pea soup and we continued to drink large quantities of tea. As far as food was concerned, if it came in tins, we had it: sausages, sardines, herrings, bacon, ox tongue, green vegetables, peas, beans, quails in truffles, sweets, crystallized ginger, figs, and prunes. There was no end of conserves and chocolate. But who enjoyed eating it? I did not. As an experienced cook, Morshead had this first rule that "the foundation of good cooking is in the stock-pot"; later on, pea soup became the base for all his dishes.

It was a point of honour to wash up, and very much may be achieved with snow. Here were the four of us fit and happy, to all appearances as we should expect to be in an alpine hut after a proper nightcap of whisky punch.

I was ready. I can still remember how my mind skimmed over the various preparations and told itself that everything was in good order, just like God after the creation. The thought of what was to come in the next two days forced its way dreamily upward, and again and again my desires soared to that highest point—ideas full of hope. My destination was extraordinarily clear: the highest point on earth!

5.19.1922

We had confidence in our porters, nine strong men willing and even keen to do whatever should be asked of them; surely these men were fit for anything. And we planned to lighten their burdens as far as possible; only four loads, beyond the warm things which each of us would carry for himself, were to go on to the next camp—two tents weighing each 15 lb., two double sleeping bags, and provisions for a day and a half besides the minimum of feeding utensils. The loads would not exceed 20 lb. each, and we should have two men to one load, and even so a man in reserve.

5.20.1922

Mallory wakes the camp early. He is impatient and wants to begin climbing soon.

It is not an enviable task at 23,000 feet, this of rousing men from the snugness of their sleeping-bags between 5 and 6 A.M. Soon I began to make out a tale of confused complaints; the porters were not all well. The cause was not far to look for; they had starved themselves of air during the night. The best chance of a remedy was fresh air now and a brew of tea, which could easily be managed.

Meanwhile, Norton had been stirring, and while I retired to "dress" he began to busy himself with preparations for our own breakfast. Tea of course was intended for us too, and further two tins of spaghetti had been reserved to give us the best possible start for the day. But one small thing had been forgotten. Those precious tins had lain all night in the snow; they should have been cuddled by human bodies, carefully nursed in the warmth of sleeping-bags. Now their contents were frozen stiff and beyond extraction even by an ice-axe. As the expenditure of treasured hot water merely for thawing spaghetti involved more melting of snow to water and boiling of water for indispensable tea, the kitchen-maid's task was disagreeably protracted; and the one among us, Norton, who most continuously and stubbornly played the man's part of kitchen-maid, sitting upon the snow in the chill early morning became a great deal colder than anyone should be with a day's mountaineering in front of him.

Of the nine porters, five suffer from altitude sickness; only four are prepared to accompany the climbers. Despite this, the team shows no evidence of world-weariness, and at 7:30 A.M. they set off. Morshead takes the lead, followed by Mallory with two porters. Norton and Somervell look after the rest, on one rope. They stand at the foot of the North Ridge and look upward.

Above the Rongbuk Glacier the broad North Flank of Everest is slightly concave in appearance; to the left, the northeastern facet is more deeply hollowed. The ground falls away more abruptly on that side below the ridge. The climber may either follow the crest of the ridge or make his way up the slopes to the right of it. The ideal line of ascent is the junction between snow and rocks, where a strip of loose stones leads up for about 450 meters at a comfortable angle. Luckily, the stones turn out to be reasonably secure, as they are bonded together by frozen snow. There is nothing more abhorrent to the climber than loose rocks giving way beneath his feet; they are almost as tiresome as knee-deep snow.

Though it can hardly be said that we enjoyed the exercise of going up Mount Everest, we were certainly

Lord Edward Felix Norton

able to enjoy the sensation so long as our progress was satisfactory. But the air remained perceptibly colder than we could have wished; and in the breeze that sprang up on our side, blowing across the ridge from the right, we recognized an enemy, the devastating wind of Tibet. We expected little mercy here, we only hoped for a period of respite.

They climb about 350 meters higher and decide to stop and put on warmer clothes: a further layer of underwear, a light woolen cardigan, and a thin silk shirt. Mallory tops it all off with his customary closely woven cotton coat. Morshead wraps a woolen scarf around his neck. When the two men are ready, they impatiently set off before the rest. Norton is sitting a little lower down, his rucksack perched on his lap, when the disaster happens:

In gathering up our rope so as to have it free when we should move on I must have communicated to the other rope some small jerk—sufficient, at all events, to upset the balance of Norton's rucksack. He was unprepared, made a desperate grab, and missed it. Slowly, the round, soft thing gathered momentum from its rotation, the first little leaps down from one ledge to another grew to excited and magnificent bounds, and the precious burden vanished from sight. . . . No one spoke. A number of offers in woolen garments for the night were soon made to Norton; after which we began to explain what each had brought for comfort's sake, and I wondered whether my companions' system of selection resembled mine.

How do I pack my rucksack? More like a gambler than a minimalist. I am not someone who likes solving puzzles. Because I never leave anything I might want behind, I first pack anything that falls into my hands. Then as if looking for a prize, I put in a hand, rummage about and pull objects out at random until the rucksack reaches the correct weight. With this process I always have sufficient spare clothing.

The sun soon disappears behind a veil of clouds. Fingertips, toes, and ears begin to suffer with the severe cold. The four men often have to seek the shelter of the leeward side of the ridge.

Mallory now takes the lead. He leaves the rocks and makes his way up and leftward over the hard snow. The angle soon increases, making steps necessary, but even with the heavy boots he is wearing he can only make a small impression in the snow. Crampons would have been useful, but they had not carried them above Camp IV. The tight straps cut off the blood supply to the feet and usually cause frostbite. Without crampons, the only way up is to cut steps.

> The proper way to cut steps in hard snow is to give one blow with the ice axe and then stamp the foot into the hole just made; but such a blow requires a man's full strength, and he must kick hard into the hole. Three hundred feet of such hard work is extremely exhausting and we were glad to finally rest at length about noon.

The pocket aneroid barometer is showing 7,600 meters compared with a reading of 7,000 on the North Col. Morshead has been delayed with some of the porters. And nowhere can they find a decent place to pitch their tents. From here on, Mallory assumes the lead.

> Among us there was deliberation often enough, but never contention. There never was a dissentient voice in anything we resolved to do, partly, I suppose, because we had little choice in the matter, more because we were that sort of party. We had a single aim in common and regarded it from common ground. We had no leader within the full meaning of the word, no one in authority over the rest to command as captain.

We all knew equally what was required to be done from first to last, and when the occasion arose for doing it one of us did it. Some one, if only to avoid delay in action, had to arrange the order in which the party or parties should proceed. I took this responsibility without waiting to be asked; the rest accepted by initiative, I suppose, because I used to talk so much about what had been done on the previous Expedition. In practice it amounted only to this, that I would say to my companions, "A, will you go first? B, will you go second?" and we roped up in the order indicated without palaver. Apart from this I never attempted to inflict my own view on men who were at least as capable as I of judging what was best. Our proceedings in any crisis of fortunes were informally democratic. . . . But we could not imagine what might be coming without thinking definitely about the porters. It would be their lot, wherever our new camp was fixed, to return this same day to Camp IV. It was no part of our design to risk even the extremities of their limbs, let alone their lives.

At about 2 P.M. Somervell finds a place to pitch a tent and immediately sets to work with a few of the porters, leveling the ground and building a supporting wall. But there is no comfortable shelf for the second tent. Each attempt by Norton and Mallory to construct their own site ends in failure. Finally, they decide to pitch their tent at the foot of a long, sloping slab. A more uncomfortable arrangement could not have been devised. One of them must lie on the slab, the other on rocks. They get little undisturbed sleep that night.

The cultured man climbs into bed, lays his head on the pillow, pulls up the covers, and falls fast asleep. At high altitudes everything is quite complex. First, there are the boots; anyone wanting to set out in the morning with warm feet and not in boots that have frozen stiff might possibly decide to sleep with his boots on or to pop them into his rucksack and use that as a pillow.

I had the tendency to slide down and . . . the pillow should be high enough if one is to breathe easily at great altitude, it was all-important . . . to make experiments in the disposition of limbs. Perhaps the fact that one was often breathless from the exhaustion of discomfort, and was obliged to breathe deeply, helped one to sleep, as deep breathing often will. I believe that both of us were sometimes unconscious in a sort of light, intermittent slumber.

As if to pass the time during the sleepless interludes, the same thought always came to mind—our plans for tomorrow. Might it not be possible to reach such and such a height in so many hours? What would happen if the day was not long enough? What for? For the summit bid of course! Because I only looked ahead instead of back, I took hope from what we had achieved so far.

The wind drops by the evening, but the clouds remain and the night is warmer than usual.

5.21.1922

In the morning, the patter of fine, granular snow can be heard on the roof of the tent. A thick mist envelops the rocks around them. At about 6:30 A.M. a break appears in the clouds. Could this be the fair day they need? "I suppose it's about time we were getting up," one among them is heard to mutter. No one disagrees. The night has been worse than the preceding day; they are more tired now than they were when they went to bed, and stiff with cold and cramp.

During the morning's preparations a second rucksack slips down the mountain, but by a miracle it stops, hung up on a ledge thirty meters below the tents. Morshead volunteers to play the rescue man and drags the heavy pack back up. At 8 A.M. the four men are ready to march and rope up, Norton first, followed by Mallory, Morshead, and Somervell.

The four men lace up their boots loosely so as to fit just tightly enough without obstructing the blood supply, and they wear their puttees just snug enough so that they do not slip down. Then they rope up, partly for convenience, so that none of them has to carry the coiled rope on his back, but also for the feeling of being united: the separate wills of individuals joined into a stronger common will. But Morshead, feeling chilled and unwell, decides to stay in camp. "I think I won't come with you any farther, I know I should only keep you back," he says. Meanwhile, Mallory is impatient to climb.

. . . it will readily be understood that there was no question for us of gymnastic struggles and strong arm-pulls, wedging ourselves in cracks and hanging on our finger-tips. We should soon have been turned back by difficulties of that sort. We could allow ourselves nothing in the nature of a violent struggle. We must avoid any hasty movement. It would have exhausted us at once to proceed by rushing up a few steps at a time. We wanted to hit off just that mean pace which we could keep up without rapidly losing our strength, to proceed evenly with balanced movements, remembering to step neatly and transfer the weight from one leg to the other by swinging the body rhythmically upwards. With the occasional help of the hands we were able to keep going for spells of twenty or thirty minutes before halting for three or four or five minutes to gather potential energy for pushing on again. Our whole power seemed to depend on the lungs. The air, such as it was, was inhaled through the mouth and expired again to some sort of tune in the unconscious mind, and the lungs beat time, as it were, for the feet. An effort of will was required not so much to induce any movement of the limbs as to set the lungs to work and keep them working.

Although they gain four hundred feet of height each hour, their progress is unsatisfactory. At 27,000 feet, they decide to turn back. It is too late in the day and a nighttime summit approach in their weakening condition would be fatal.

Mallory decides they should now get back to Morshead in time to take him down to Camp IV. They start down at 2:30 P.M.

It is impossible to say how much more we could have achieved. In the light of later experiences, and compared with what Jon Krakauer has to say, I believe I am right in saying that the reserves we had available for any unforeseen eventualities were too limited. We might perhaps have been able to slog our way up to the northeast shoulder over the next two hours. Whether we would then still have been capable of climbing down again is another matter.

The only food they have is chocolate, biscuits, raisins, and prunes. Knowing their bodies need nourishment despite their lack of appetite, they choke every mouthful down. One of them produces a bottle of cognac from his pocket and they all take a nip. It gives them the necessary energy for the descent.

Norton and Mallory now swap places on the rope and Mallory takes over the lead. At 4 P.M. they reach the camp, where Morshead is waiting. After gathering a few items they continue down.

I sometimes wonder what an independent observer would have had to say about our performance that day. Without a doubt our creeping upward progress would have given him grave cause for concern. Nevertheless, at that stage each of us was still in control of his limbs and sense of balance. Then suddenly that all changed. When we set off from Camp V, all our reserves of strength were suddenly exhausted and we were less attentive.

The fresh snow that had fallen overnight, their exhaustion, and their inattentiveness add to the risk of the descent. Suddenly, the third man slips and pulls the last man off balance. The second in the party tries to brake but cannot arrest their fall and is dragged off with them. The three of them slip down the slope with gathering speed, heading straight for a precipice and a thousand-meter drop to the East Rongbuk Glacier.

Only Mallory manages to stay on his feet. As soon as he hears suspicious noises behind him, he rams his ax deep into the snow, whips the rope around it, leans his whole weight on it, and braces himself for the pull. The rope comes taut, gives a little, creaks, and—holds. The party proceeds with extra caution after this incident.

5.22.1922

The men continue down to Camp III together. There is no sign of their old tracks, and on the steep sections new steps have to be cut in the hard snow below the fresh surface. At the foot of the ice wall, the lead man decides it would be more companionable for them all to finish together. As he turns, he carelessly slips. Mallory is pulled from his steps and dragged twenty-five meters down before his ice-ax brake works.

Mallory is astonished at all the commotion at the foot of the North Col.

Finch was now testing the oxygen apparatus with Wakefield and Geoffrey Bruce. They were bound for the North Col with a party of porters.

George Ingle Finch, a chemist by profession, is one of the most experienced British mountaineers of the day, and a man accustomed to unguided climbing. He advocates the use of oxygen on Everest, a cause he espouses with vigor. Finch will

Testing the oxygen equipment in 1922

attempt a second assault with two men who have little idea of mountaineering matters: Captain Geoffrey Bruce, a nephew of General Bruce, and Tedjbir Bura, an officer in the Gurkhas. At Camp III both men are instructed by Finch in the use of crampons, ice axes, and ropes.

5.24.1922

The oxygen apparatus has suffered during transport across Tibet, and only at Camp III is Finch able to effect emergency repairs. Finch's party moves up to Camp IV with all the available high-altitude porters. Captain J. B. Noel, the expedition cameraman, accompanies them as far as the North Col.

5.25.1922

The weather breaks and the intended high camp at around 8,100 meters cannot be established, but Finch does not give up. A tent is hastily pitched at 7,770 meters, on a little ledge on the backbone of the ridge, with no protection from the wind. The storm rages and it starts to snow. During the night, the wind rises to hurricane force and continues unabated for eighteen hours. Retreat to the North Col is out of the question.

5.27.1922

After a second night at Camp V, Finch and Bruce resume their assault. The weather is clear, windy, and fiercely cold.

Tedjbir, with two extra bottles of compressed oxygen, has twenty-three kilograms on his back. At an altitude of 7,925 meters he collapses, exhausted, and returns to Camp V. But still Finch and Bruce do not give up. They follow the crest of

THE SECOND DEATH OF GEORGE MALLORY

the ridge upward, but the wind increases in force and they have to strike out to the right across the north face of the mountain. They manage to reach a height of 8,326 meters despite the fresh snow and a broken connection in Bruce's oxygen mask. Taking only short breaks, Finch and Bruce then descend two thousand meters back to Camp III. By the time they get there, they are totally spent.

6.5.1922

Mallory decides to make one last attempt.

> The weather on the morning of June 5 improved and we decided to go on. Low and heavy clouds were still flowing down the east Rongbuk Glacier, but precipitation ceased at an early hour and the sky brightened to the West. We were well up towards Camp III before the fresh snow became a serious impediment. It was still snowing up here, though not very heavily; there was nothing to cheer the grey scene. Camp III . . . had first to be dug out.

6.6.1922

They are hesitant about making a third attempt. Would there be any avalanche danger higher up? But the morning breaks fine:

> As we watched the amazing rapidity with which the snow solidified and the rocks began to appear about our camp, our spirits rose. We had already resolved

View of Mount Everest from the Rongbuk Monastery

to use oxygen on our third attempt. All those who had used oxygen were convinced that they went up more easily with its help than they could expect to go without it. Somervell and I intended to profit by their experience. They had discovered that the increased combustion in the body required a larger supply of food; we must arrange for a bountiful supply.

6.7.1922

At 8 A.M., Somervell, Crawford, Mallory, and fourteen porters set out. In spite of the hard frost of the previous night, the snow crust does not bear their weight; they sink up to their knees with every step. The three climbers move without loads and have to take turns stamping out the track for their porters. In this way, they work their way up the steep snow slope.

It was necessarily slow work forging our way through the deep snow, but the party was going extraordinarily well, and the porters were evidently determined to get on. Somervell gave us a long lead, and Crawford next, in spite of the handicap of shorter legs, struggled upwards in some of the worst snow we met until I relieved him. . . . It was necessary to pause after each lifting movement for a whole series of breaths, rapid at first and gradually slower, before the weight was transferred again to the other foot. . . . We were now about 600 feet below Camp IV. The scene was particularly bright and windless, nothing was to be heard but the laboured panting of our lungs. This stillness was suddenly disturbed. We were startled by an ominous sound; all of us, I imagine, knew instinctively what it meant.

Without warning, a snow-slab avalanche sweeps the climbing party down toward the abyss. Seven porters die. This accident ends the third attempt.

It might be supposed that, from the experience of two expeditions to Mount Everest, it would be possible to deduce an estimate of the dangers and difficulties involved and to formulate a plan. . . . In fact, I should be surprised to find anything like complete agreement. One thing is certain: the final camp was too low. The aim . . . must be to establish a camp considerably higher than our camp at 25,000 feet and two camps instead of one must be placed above the Chang La; another stage must be added to the structure before the climbing party sets forth to reach the summit. One of the physiologists who has been most deeply concerned with this problem of acclimatisation considers that it would probably be desirable to stay four or five days at 25,000 feet before proceeding to attempt the last two stages on consecutive days. But, the increasing desire to get away from Camp V might lead to retreat instead of advance. The conditions at the top camp must be altogether more comfortable if the aspiring climbers are to derive any advantage from their rustication at this altitude.

Mallory understands that properly supplying the camps and improving the quality of the climbing equipment would be essential to a successful summit assault. Their footwear especially needs improvement. Mallory is the first to recognize the danger of frostbite from the boots and crampons they wear. Even more critical are modifications to the oxygen apparatus. In 1922, a climber would carry four steel cylinders to the summit and back. A new type of cylinder, lighter and capable of containing more oxygen, would prove an invaluable asset to a summit team.

3.18.1923
Back home in England, Mallory announces both his failure and the start of the next expedition. In an unsigned article in

the *New York Times* under the title "The Ascent of Mount Everest—a Job for Superman," Mallory is quoted as planning to return in 1924. In answer to the question about the reason for his repeated attempts to reach the summit of Everest, he replies, "Because it is there."

CHAPTER FOUR

1924: THE SECOND STEP

*The Second Step; today's climbers avoid it on
the right*

We were a sad little party; from the first we accepted the loss of our comrades in that rational spirit which all of our generation had learnt in the Great War, and there was never any tendency to a morbid harping on the irrevocable. But the tragedy was very near; our friends' vacant tents and vacant places at table were a constant reminder to us of what the atmosphere of the camp would have been had things gone differently. To several of us, particularly to those who, on previous expeditions to Mount Everest or Spitzbergen, had been close friends with the missing climbers, the sense of loss was acute and personal. . . . [Mallory's] death had robbed us of a right loyal friend, a knight amongst mountaineers and the greatest antagonist that Everest has had—or is likely to have.

—Edward Felix Norton

TO SUFFICIENTLY PREPARE for the next attempt, the British Everest Committee decides to wait until 1924 to mount the Third Expedition. And this time, it is to be conclusive. For a successful ascent, they decide that the oxygen apparatus must be improved and a new type of cylinder constructed, a third lighter than the old version. Above all, warmer and more windproof clothing must be developed, to offer protection against the dreadful storms on Mount Everest.

The participants of the big 1924 expedition are the most experienced and talented climbers available. General Charles G. Bruce is the leader of the group with Edward Felix Norton as his first lieutenant. Mallory, Somervell, Odell (a geologist), Irvine, Beetham, Hazard, and Geoffrey Bruce are the lead climbers. Hingston, the expedition doctor, Noel, the cameraman, and two officers in charge of transport round out the team.

Norton has got the whole organization under his hand, and . . . the party looks very fit altogether. We had a very hot journey through India. The hot weather apparently came with a rush this year just before we landed. It's a grim and dusty business, and I was glad to get to the end of our train journeying. Four of us walked up to Seneschal Hill yesterday afternoon to see the magnolias—I was trying out my new boots from Dewberry; they are going to be good. The magnolias were magnificent—a better show than last year—four different sorts, white and deep cerise pink and two lighter pinks between— they do look startlingly bright on a dark hillside. The country here is very dry at present and a haze of dust blown up from the plains hangs about. Kanchen has very dimly made an appearance.

Tomorrow we go to Kalimpong all together, as before, and then separate in two parties; I shall be with the second, with Norton, Hingston, Irvine and Shebbeare, I believe. Noel's movements are independent.

The English mail should have come in yesterday, but the ship was twelve hours late and we shan't get it until today and consequently will have precious little time for answering.

3.25.1924

Their huge caravan sets off from Darjeeling. More than 350 horses, mules, donkeys, oxen, and yaks carry the expedition's luggage, while the climbers ride in cars for the first ten kilometers. The unwieldy train of baggage and the climbers in cars progress across the well-known route over the high Tibetan plains. On the way, a tea planter named Lister Norton invites Somervell and Mallory to breakfast. Owner of the most famous tea gardens in Sikkim, he serves the climbers delicacies they will not have again for a while. Marring this promising beginning is the sudden illness of General Bruce. Due to the seriousness of his malaria attack, Bruce is immediately sent back to Sikkim. Norton takes over the lead and names Mallory as his second-in-command and leader of the climbers.

4.7.1924

Each team member has a Whymper tent to himself. This type of tent has two poles at each end and is therefore considerably more roomy than tents with single poles. Mallory is especially pleased with the "ground-sheet sewn into the sides so that draught and dust are practically excluded if one pitches in the right direction; and, a great blessing, the tent has plenty of pockets. Moreover, it is by no means small—7 feet square or very near it."

Mallory adjusts better than he did in 1921 and 1922 to the high altitude. He manages as well uphill as he does in the Alps and is sleeping soundly.

The weather, however, is a constant concern. Although all of the reports promised clear skies, the air is heavy with moisture. The team fears that an unexpected monsoon could destroy their chance for a successful ascent.

4.14.1924

For the summit assault, Norton proposes two plans. First, that two men without oxygen should establish Camp V at 8,100 meters and attempt the summit the following day. Or second, that on the day the two climbers leave Camp V, a party of three arrive in Camp V with oxygen and wait for the return of the first two climbers before making their own attempt.

The advantage of the second plan is that the two groups can support each other. The disadvantage is that the rope of two will have to make do with only one camp, whereas the best chance of success would be with two camps between the North Col and the summit. If the gasless attempt fails and the climbers "on gas" are also unsuccessful, two men have been unnecessarily wasted.

> *Norton and I worked together in complete harmony. As I was learning Hindi and trying to get to know all the names of the Sherpas, there was little time left for reading. From time to time I managed to lose myself in the letters of Keats or in "Spirit of Man." As if an unknown destiny was within me, I was afraid of responsibility. And I was indeed convinced that from now on I would remain healthy, but not certain what the outcome would be this time. We can master the mountain but not our own destiny. I pondered the great ascent incessantly, the last attempt.*

4.17.1924

Mallory proposes an alternative to Norton's plans. First, starting from Camp IV, climbers A and B with fifteen porters establish Camp V at 25,500 feet and descend. Next, climbers C and D, without oxygen, go to Camp V with another fifteen porters. Seven of the porters carry loads, then descend, while the other eight go up without loads and remain in camp overnight. The next day, C and D establish Camp VI at 27,300 with eight porters, only six carrying loads. At the same time, climbers E and F start from Camp IV with ten porters. Using oxygen, E and F take on the supplies dumped at Camp V and climb on to Camp VI. The next morning, the two parties begin the summit ascent.

To Mallory, the merits of this plan are manifold:

> There is the mutual support which the two parties can give each other; the establishment of camps without waste of reserve climbers (A and B will not have done so much that they can't recover); the much better chance this way of establishing VI without collapse of porters. And then if this go fails we shall be in the best possible position to decide how the next attempt should be made; four climbers we hope will be available and the camps either way will all be ready.

> *While formulating this plan, I was ruled by feelings of doubt and fear. My responsibility to myself, the team, and the mountain weighed heavily on me.*

Norton and I have talked about it; he thinks Somervell and I should each lead one of these two parties; he puts himself in my hands as to whether he should be one of them—isn't that generous? We shall have to judge as best we can of people's fitness when we reach Base Camp. Either Odell or Irvine must be of the gas party.

4.22.1924

Mallory and Norton spend all their spare time perfecting the climbing plan. After prolonged consultation, Norton makes a general announcement after dinner. Mallory will lead the oxygen party (E and F) and be responsible for the descent of both teams. Either Odell or Irvine will accompany him due to their expertise with the oxygen equipment. Somervell and Norton will make the gasless attempt.

It is difficult to deny certain people a chance at reaching the summit in order for the overall mission to be a success. Mallory admits, "The whole difficulty of fitting people in so that they take part in an assault according to their desire or ambition is so great that I can't feel distressed about the part that falls to me."

Mallory is pleased with the role he will play in the assault and is confident that Irvine will make a reliable companion.

4.24.1924

Two days later, Mallory writes to his wife:

My plan will be to carry as little as possible . . . Finch and Bruce tried carrying too many cylinders.

And I have very good hopes that the gasless party

will get up; I want all four of us to get there, and I believe it can be done. We shall be starting by moon-
light if the morning is calm and should have the
mountain climbed if we're lucky before the wind is
dangerous. . . . On May 17, or thereabouts, we should
reach the summit. I'm eager for the great events to
begin.

At the end of April, Base Camp is finally established in the
Rongbuk Valley. The weather is good and everyone is full of
confidence. Although the lower slopes of Mount Everest look
quite white, it is dark above. In fact, even after a snowfall the
summit area hardly ever looks any different. There is no time
to lose now; the establishment of the high camps much start
without delay.

4.27.1924
Mallory organizes the equipment for the high camps and
arranges for the loads to be carried up.

Establishing Camp III is particularly critical because it will
supply Camp IV. Mallory also drafts a load plan. His sugges-
tions are intricate but allow plenty of leeway, so that even two
days of bad weather will not thwart his plans.

> *The farther we are from the mountain, the more it seems
> like the end of the world.*

Searching for a new route always takes more time than
climbing an old one. Feeling mildly unwell, Mallory only just

Andrew "Sandy" Irvine on the 1924 Everest expedition

makes it to Camp III. Arriving at the old camp, Mallory is re-minded of that last tragic expedition two years ago. The rusty oxygen bottles piled against the cairn remain in commemora-tion of the seven porters killed. The rest of the camp is also eerily unchanged.

The porters struggle to reach the camp. By 6 P.M. it is al-ready bitterly cold.

5.7.1924

Mallory looks overtired, and the other team members won-der if he will be able to successfully complete the assault.

5.8.1924

To lighten Mallory's burden, Geoffrey Bruce is placed in charge of the tents, the welfare of the porters, and the daily or-ders. Mallory gets up early again and goes up to Camp II, where he meets Norton and Somervell. He is visibly relieved that the responsibility does not rest solely on his shoulders. Mallory, Norton, and Bruce escort three of the porters to Camp III.

At Camp III, Mallory shares a tent with Somervell. Decid-ing to rest in the tent after the long trek, he takes off his boots and trousers and puts on footless stockings, gray flannel trousers, two pairs of socks, cloth-sided shoes, and an extra jumper before slipping into his sleeping bag. Only then is he ready to play a game of piquet with Somervell.

Later, Norton and Bruce join Mallory and Somervell in their tent to discuss the next day's challenges. For inspiration, Mallory reads aloud from "The Spirit of Man." Somervell reminds him that they did exactly the same thing two years ago when they shared a tent.

During the night a storm hits the camp. The wind comes in hefty gusts, blowing ice-cold spindrift through the seams of the tents. In the morning, they find two inches of snow in the tent; everything is clammy and cold. Outside, there is more new snow and violent wind. Should they retreat? Mallory is against the idea. He wants to wait it out for another day. Norton concurs, and they agree that Somervell, Norton, and Odell will try to push the route to the North Col while Mallory and Irvine return to Base Camp.

5.11.1924

Back at Base Camp, Mallory and Irvine learn that Norton has decided to evacuate Camp III and recall everyone to Base. It is the first setback. The mountain is showing its teeth.

5.27.1924

On the second foray, conditions at Camp III are again hellish, with biting cold and high winds. Hopes are fading fast. Yet Norton and Mallory still manage to fight their way up to the North Col, fixing ropes on the ice wall and the Chimney Pitch. On the descent, Mallory falls into a snowy crevasse, luckily coming to a stop after about three meters as his ice ax jams across the rift. "Below me was a very unpleasant black hole," he recalls. The others have no idea where he might be and so he has no choice but to scrape at the snow to enlarge the hole and crawl out of the crevasse. He is also suffering with a cough. At the higher camps this makes his life a misery, and a violent fit of coughing up at the North Col almost tears his guts out. With their impaired physical condition and the impending monsoon, will they get the chance to mount another assault?

The whole team is in a sorry state. The men must try to recover as best they can and then implement a simpler, quicker plan of assault. Norton leaves the choice of the next wave of troops to Mallory. He decides Norton and Somervell should make the summit attempt.

May is generally considered a good-weather month on Everest, but in 1924 it is as cold as winter with a lot of precipitation. At Camp III the thermometer falls to thirty degrees below zero, and twice the team has to be recalled to Base Camp. These two retreats are beset with storms and avalanche danger and cost two Sherpas their lives. Sahibs and porters alike are growing weary.

6.1.1924

All the camps below the North Col are now occupied, and Camp IV is established on the Col. Beyond the Col the porter loads must not exceed nine kilograms, so Somervell and Norton carry rucksacks with their personal effects.

Norton is dressed in thick woolen underwear, a thick flannel shirt, and two jumpers. On top of this he wears a mountain suit made from windproof gabardine, the breeches of which are lined in flannel, and puttees made of soft cashmere wool. The leather soles of his felt boots are specially made for mountaineering but are not too heavily nailed. Over all of this he wears a full-length windproof suit in Burberry's

Climbing the Ice Chimney on the Chang La face

"Shackleton Wind Gabardine." His hands are covered by long woolen mittens with gabardine overgloves, and on his head he wears a fur-lined leather helmet of the type then common among motorcyclists. His snow goggles are sewn into a leather mask, which covers the part of his face unprotected by his beard, and a broad woolen neck-warmer completes the ensemble. Somervell is dressed in a similar fashion. For a better grip when cutting steps, they both exchange their woolen mittens for silk gloves. Even the porters are equipped with windsuits and woolen clothing.

They follow the old route along the North Ridge.

6.2.1924

Mallory and Bruce arrive at 7,700 meters with their porters, but violent wind prevents further progress. They decide to descend with two of Norton's porters. Norton, Somervell, and four porters eventually reach Camp V without any further problems.

The afternoon is spent as normal. The two climbers rest in their sleeping bags. Eventually, one drags himself, gasping, to the nearest patch of snow and fills the aluminum pots. Meanwhile, the other man sits up in bed, groaning, and sets up the meta burner. From the bags of pemmican, tea, sugar, milk, powder, sardines, and crackers, he takes what he thinks they need, and both men settle down in their sleeping bags to wait for the meta cooker to heat the snow into lukewarm water. At such altitudes the kitchen work is as strenuous as climbing—and less satisfying. Solid food is unappetizing at these heights, and no matter how much liquid is consumed, it never feels like enough.

6.3.1924

The two men get up at 5 A.M. While Somervell busies himself preparing breakfast, Norton checks on the porters' tent; they should make themselves some tea and have something to eat. Two of them appear to be injured. Only Lhakpa Chedi looks fit to walk. And as for Narbu Jischee? Norton gives a sermon about honor and heroism: just six hundred meters more and they will have carried their loads five hundred meters higher than any other man. Norton perseveres and soon three high-altitude porters are ready to do one more uphill stage—but only with nine-kilogram loads.

At about midday, they pass the highest point reached by Mallory, Somervell, and Norton in 1922. At 1:30 P.M. they establish Camp VI at 8,150 meters on a little rock niche facing north. It provides adequate shelter from the violent northwest wind. Once the tent is pitched, Norton inspects the route, while the porters descend to the camp at the North Col. Norton and Somervell spend the night at Camp VI alone. As Norton later recounts:

> The altitude of Camp VI is later calculated to be
> 8,145 meters; this is the highest camp anyone has so
> far spent a night in. Most of the physiologists had pre-
> viously considered this impossible.

Nevertheless, it is the best night's sleep Norton has had since Camp I.

6.4.1924

Norton and Somervell begin their summit assault at 6:40 A.M. There is virtually no wind—an ideal day, of the kind only rarely found on the upper reaches of Mount Everest.

An hour above camp, Norton and Somervell come across a layer of sandstone running right across the northern flank of Everest; progress is easier across these long sloping terraces. This Yellow Band is composed of calcareous sandstone and loose sandstone slabs like tiles on a roof; it runs across the north face of the massif and forms a long system of ledges that, as long as they remain free of snow, are easy to climb. Nevertheless, the two climbers make only slow progress due to the lack of oxygen—they are climbing without breathing apparatus. After every few steps they stop for a rest; Somervell is suffering from a racking cough caused by the thin, dry air, and Norton is shivering with cold even when resting in the sun. Norton only wears his snow goggles when actually on the snowed-up sections, which occur only irregularly, since the rims of the goggles limit his field of vision when searching for footholds. At 8,400 meters his eyes suddenly start giving him trouble; he begins to have double vision and is uncertain where to place his feet. Is he going snow-blind? Somervell says no; it is out of the question. So it must just be hallucinations caused by oxygen deficiency. The two men can now only manage about twenty paces before stopping and gasping for air. At noon, Norton and Somervell are at the upper edge of the Yellow Band, near the big gully that runs down the huge north face. Somervell's throat complaint is now so bad that he is forced to give up, and he remains behind. Despite violent bouts of shivering and choking fits he still manages, at a height of 8,540 meters, to take that famous photograph of a lone Norton heading toward the summit of Everest, which soars above him like an arrow piercing the sky (see page 158).

> *Shortly after a late breakfast, whilst Sandy and I were preparing the oxygen apparatus for our attempt, a porter came down and told us that Somervell and Norton had established Camp VI and had spent the night there. Although hoping that they would succeed, even Sandy was concerned we might be too late.*

Norton is now high above all the other peaks—to the north, the mountains of Tibet are ranged before him—and the terrain below appears to be flat. He has lost all sense of distance. Far in the background he sees a row of ice domes, one behind the other, but otherwise everything is hazy.

As he approaches the Great Couloir, the terrain becomes more difficult. Powdery snow conceals the narrow foothold ledges. For a well-acclimatized climber, Norton makes painfully slow progress. Norton is straining every last muscle to succeed. The grip of his nailed boots on the smooth, snow-covered limestone slabs is unpredictable, his nerves are strained to the breaking point, and he is exhausted. In addition, his eye trouble, caused by lack of oxygen, is getting worse. In an hour, he only manages to go two hundred and seventy meters and gains only thirty meters in vertical height.

At the end of his physical endurance, Norton must still

scale three hundred meters of vertical height to reach the summit. These three hundred meters, the height of the Eiffel Tower, will take hours of hard work and concentration to scale. Norton is left with no choice: If he does not wish to die, he must turn back.

The descent route, first back down to Somervell, who loses his ice ax, and then back down the way they have come, is successfully accomplished. At Camp VI they collect a few things and grab a tent pole as a replacement ice ax, collapse the tent, and weight it down with stones. Then they head down to Camp IV.

They pass by Camp V as the sun is setting, climbing un-roped. Somervell lags behind and nearly chokes during a coughing fit. Moving by the light of a pocket flashlight and by now completely dehydrated, they are within reach of Camp IV at the North Col when Mallory sees them coming: "As they came back down, Odell and I went to meet them. They were a sorry sight. Both men were at the end of their tether, both physically and psychologically, and Norton was snow-blind. I now knew—and this decision was final—that Irvine and I would climb with oxygen apparatus."

Now I was under pressure to move; Norton had failed in his attempt without oxygen, and I knew I had to act quickly if my attempt was to be successful. It was now or never.

6.9.1924

Hazard and Odell train their field glasses on the tents at the high camp. It has been four days since Mallory and Irvine left camp for their assault attempt, and the team is getting worried. They should have been back by now.

Toward midday, Odell decides to set off for Camp V. He devises a simple signaling system with Hazard: During daylight hours he will lay sleeping bags out in the snow in a predetermined pattern, at night he will flash his flashlight. Odell sets off at midday with two porters. A bitterly cold west wind whistles across the slopes of the mountain. Nevertheless, Odell climbs on, continuing the search.

Camp V is deserted.

6.10.1924

The porters, suffering from altitude sickness, descend in the morning to the North Col. Odell climbs on alone to Camp VI. With the help of oxygen he makes good progress. From time to time, however, he seeks the shelter of the rocks to warm himself up again. Before reaching Camp VI he concludes that the oxygen really is of little use:

> Within an hour or so of Camp VI, I came to the conclusion that I was deriving but little benefit from the oxygen, which I had been taking only in moderate quantities from the single cylinder that I carried. I gave myself larger quantities and longer inspirations of it, but the effect seemed almost negligible: perhaps it just allayed a trifle the tire in one's legs. I wondered at the claims of others regarding its advantages, and could only conclude that I was fortunate in having

acclimatized myself more thoroughly to the air of these altitudes and to its small percentage of available oxygen. I switched the oxygen off and experienced none of those feelings of collapse and panting that one had been led to believe ought to result. I decided to proceed with the apparatus on my back, but without the objectionable rubber mouthpiece between my lips, and depend on direct breathing from the atmosphere. I seemed to get on quite well, though I must admit the hard breathing at these altitudes would surprise even a long-distance runner.

The tent at Camp VI is exactly as Norton and Somervell had left it. Two days have passed since the storm on the summit.

Odell climbs on, searching, shouting, but the wind rages over the mountain, smothering every sound. He has never been so cold or so lonely. This is a bitter loss.

There is nothing he can do alone. A thorough search would require a rescue party. Odell sums it all up thus:

After struggling on for nearly a couple of hours looking in vain for some indication or clue, I realized that the chances of finding the missing ones were indeed small on such a vast expanse of crags and broken slabs, and that for any more extensive search towards the final pyramid a further party would have to be organized. At the same time I considered, and still do consider, that wherever misfortune befell them some traces of them would be discovered on or near the ridge of the North-east Arête: I saw them on that ridge on the morning of their ascent and presumably they would descend by it. But in the time available under the prevailing conditions, I found it impossible to extend my search.

In deep thought, Odell begins the descent. He wonders, "Why did they never get back to the tent at Camp VI? Were they unable to find it in the dark? If Mallory was leading, he must have fallen, since Irvine would not have been able to pull him off if he were belayed." Only the chill wind shakes Odell out of his gloomy thoughts.

At the North Col he finds a note from Norton, consoling him and assuring him that Odell has done all he can. The monsoon might begin any moment.

Odell takes two sleeping bags—the sleeping bags that Mallory and Irvine had left behind at Camp VI—and spreads them out on a patch of snow. From below, Noel observes two little black lines; they form a *T*. It means "nothing found." Norton replies by arranging three blankets in the shape of a cross: "break off the search." The distant messages have an air of finality about them.

Odell takes Mallory's compass and the oxygen breather that Irvine had built and closes the tent flap. The clouds chase across the mountain; for a moment the summit is revealed, then the clouds cover it once more. Odell is racked with questions concerning his lost friends. What could have gone so horribly wrong? "If it were indeed the holy ground of

The memorial pyramid at Everest Base Camp, 1924

Chomolungma, had we violated it—was I now violating it?"
Odell later asks himself. "There seemed to be something al-
luring in that towering presence" is his answer. "I realized
that . . . he who approaches close must ever be led on, and
oblivious of all obstacles seek to reach that most sacred and
highest place of all. It seems that my friends must have been
thus enchanted also: for why else should they tarry?"

"It was just chance that I took out to the Alps in 1904 a
boy destined to become so famous upon Everest," Mallory's
mountaineering companion R. L. G. Irvine later relates, seeing in this young man first a callow youth, inexperienced in
the ways of climbing, and then his best pupil. Mallory was at
that time a good sportsman and in particular a brilliant gym-
nast. On the first alpine peak they climbed together, Mallory
promptly got altitude sickness at a height of barely 3,500 meters, yet his talent had been discovered. "He was a beautiful
climber, with such good balance that any movement was
made with the least possible effort." What Mr. G. W. Young
has said in a great tribute to that acknowledged prince among
guides, Franz Lochmatter—"I never saw him 'struggle' "—
might have been said of Mallory. Climbing with him was in-
separable from artistry. No man living has a better knowledge
of the Everest expedition than Colonel E. F. Norton, and in
his opinion Mallory was the greatest antagonist Everest has
had—or is likely to have.

6.13.1924

Everyone is back at Base Camp. A memorial is built from
stones and slabs of rock. A brief high summer has come to the

valley beneath the big mountain. The hills are a delicate shade of green, and butterflies fly in the sun-filled air. Birds nest between the stones. The world is suddenly full of voices.

6.15.1924

The last of the pack animals leaves the Camp. Solitude, silence, and harmony remain.

CHAPTER FIVE

1933: THE ICE AX

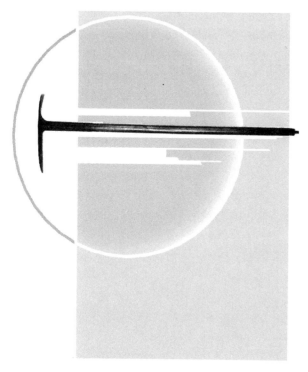

The ice ax found in 1933

Wyn Harris and Wager intended to reach the crest of
the ridge, and, as Mallory had purposed, proceed along
it to the final pyramid and up that to the summit, 1,600
feet above their camp, and about a mile and a quarter
distant.

—SIR FRANCIS YOUNGHUSBAND

I assume without hesitation that the attempt to climb
Mount Everest will be continued. We cannot leave the
work unfinished.

—HUGH RUTTLEDGE

The summit pyramid of Mount Everest, viewed from about 8,300 meters

1. Route of ascent via the slabs of the Yellow Band
2. Wager reaches the ridge here
3. Ice ax found here (1933)
4. First Step
5. Second Step
6. Highest point reached in 1924 and 1933 (8,565 meters)
7. The Great Couloir

4.19.1933

It has taken nine years for the Dalai Lama to grant approval for a new Everest expedition. The participants of the earlier expeditions are all now either dead or too old, so a young, strong team is assembled. Base Camp and the first four high camps are established at the previous sites.

The weather is especially unforgiving this year. Expedition leader Hugh Ruttledge reports that a powerful stream of cold air routinely hinders progress. Every step uphill is torturous. Eyes burn despite the snow goggles, limbs are limp and lifeless. Worst is the icy air that pierces the lungs.

5.26.1933

An assault plan is finally devised.

5.28.1933

Hopes are high. The weather seems to be breaking and the climbers hope that the milder premonsoon period is beginning. Wyn Harris and Wager, members of the lead team, set off from the North Col with twelve porters, whom they refer to as the "tigers." They bivouac at Camp V for the night and fill their thermos with hot tea for breakfast the next morning.

5.29.1933

Departure is at 8 A.M. Eight "tigers" declare themselves ready to continue the climb. Wyn Harris and Wager take the lead. They alternate fifty minutes of climbing with ten minutes of rest and climb an average of 120 meters an hour.

At an altitude of 8,357 meters, the group establishes Camp VI among some steep, slabby crags. A platform is constructed and the little tent, seven feet long and four feet wide, is pitched as securely as possible. Four sleeping bags and food for four days are put inside, as well as cooking equipment and stoves.

The "tigers" return to Camp V. Harris and Wager remain. A snowstorm breaks unexpectedly. The howling wind and lashing snow prevent much-needed sleep.

5.30.1933

Harris and Wager do not make a good start. With no sleep, no appetite, and raging thirst, they are not in ideal condition. For a whole hour they melt snow on one stove while thawing their frozen climbing boots over a second. Once those tasks are complete, they begin the ascent.

Their clothing is standard expedition issue for those days: a Shetland-wool vest, a thick flannel shirt, a camel-hair sweater, six lightweight Shetland pullovers, two pairs of Shetland long

Harris and Wager above Camp VI

johns, four pairs of Shetland stockings, flannel trousers, and as a top layer, a semi-silk Grenfell windsuit. On his head, each wears a light balaclava helmet, beneath a Grenfell canvas cap. The big mountain boots are only lightly nailed, but provide good traction on steep slopes. They wear fingerless woolen mittens and a pair of overgloves made from South African lamb's wool.

Like their predecessors, the climbers must first reach the ridge. Since the sun is not yet shining onto the north side, they suffer badly from the cold for the first hour or so. They lose body heat quickly due to hyperventilation (the short, gasping breaths caused by the lack of oxygen at this altitude), and the early signs of hypothermia are soon recognizable.

Nevertheless, they press on following Mallory's plan of climbing to the summit pyramid. The summit itself is still a mile and a half (2.2 kilometers) from the last camp, and up 480 meters.

As the first chill rays of sun hit them, Harris, who is in the lead, stops briefly. Something is lying on the slanting rock ledge in front of him. He goes over, picks it up, and examines it closely. It is an ice ax with nick marks on the handle. It could only have belonged to Mallory or Irvine. They wonder if they are standing at the scene of the 1924 tragedy. They examine the immediate area for further clues—oxygen bottles, a second ax, a body. Nothing else is found.

I came to rest much farther down so they can't see me.

Continuing their ascent, Harris and Wager leave the ice ax behind. They fear it will bring bad luck. They decide to retrieve it on their way back down from the summit.

They turn the First Step—two wide rock towers on the ridge. Beyond it, the Northeast Ridge still looks difficult. Progress is slow.

Harris and Wager follow the route Norton and Somervell took in 1924 along the flank of the mountain. This route too is as difficult as it is dangerous, with snow-covered ledges and slabs of rock arranged in layers, like roofing slates. Below are a vertical precipice and a bottomless abyss. A fall from here would end on the glacier three thousand meters below. Rounding a corner, they see an enormous snow couloir running down from the summit pyramid. Powder snow here too.

At twelve-thirty, three hundred meters below the summit, and at roughly the same height Norton reached in 1924, they give up. They need time for the descent. When they arrive back at Camp IV at four o'clock in the afternoon, Frank S. Smythe and Eric E. Shipton have already arrived. They show them the ice ax.

The stray ice ax is exhibited in England like an ancient relic, put on display for the world to see. It is given a place of honor next to a photograph of me in the Alpine Club in London.

All that remains of the missing Mallory/Irvine partnership is the ice ax. Although it is only five hundred meters in vertical height from the last camp to the summit, Harris and Wager conclude that the ridge is unclimbable because of the steepness of the Second Step.

6.1.1933

Smythe and Shipton set off from the top camp. Shipton soon returns to Camp VI, complaining of stomach pain. Smythe carries on alone and at ten o'clock he reaches the same place on the ridge where Harris and Wager were forced to turn back. Poor conditions and the lack of oxygen force Smythe, one of the best of the English climbers, to retreat as well. Without oxygen, Smythe suffers from hallucinations. He believes a second person is on the rope with him and that should he fall, this second man would hold him. At his high-point, 8,572 meters above sea level, he breaks a biscuit in two, turns—and is shocked to find that he is alone. During the descent, just before Camp VI, the bond between him and "the

Wyn Harris and Wager on Mount Everest

other man" is abruptly broken. Smythe suddenly feels lonely and miserable, in spite of his setting an altitude record.

Reaching the summit alone would surely have brought fame, but wouldn't reasonable opinion support helping the injured party down? Climbers must always check their ambition with compassion.

CHAPTER SIX

1953: THE ASCENT FROM THE SOUTH

Edmund Hillary (right) and Tensing Norgay,
the first men to climb Mount Everest

The desire to see the world beats in my heart. You look to the West. I want to go East. Go back if you can. I will go back if I wish.

—Arnolt Bronnen

The Southeast Ridge of Mount Everest from the South Summit

5.26.1953

Twenty years after Smythe and Shipton, a British team led by John Hunt approach the summit from the southern side of Nepal. The team includes, among others, Bourdillon, Evans, New Zealander Edmund Hillary, and Sherpa Tensing Norgay. Establishing their camp at 8,504 meters, higher than that of the 1933 expedition, proves the key to success.

Nine expedition members get as far as the South Col, three of them twice. Seven of the nine make it to 8,200 meters; four manage to climb the 8,760-meter South Summit. Of the twenty-seven original Sherpas, nineteen climb as far as the South Col, six of them twice.

5.28.1953

Bourdillon and Evans failed to reach the South Summit on May 26. Hillary and Tensing prepare to ascend the summit the next day.

5.29.1953

Hillary and Tensing emerge from their tent at 6:30 A.M. By nine they have reached the South Summit, and by eleven they are on the last steep step. Hillary examines the difficult path ahead. The belay ledge is dangerously narrow. Looking straight down into the Western Cwm, he can see Camp IV. They decide Tensing should belay first. Hillary scrapes out handholds from an ice bulge hanging down from the last rock step. This is the last major obstacle before the summit—success is critical. Luckily the weather is good and their nerve is strong. They continue up slowly.

> *The Southern Ridge—ay me. If only I had attempted the summit from the south, I am almost certain I would have been successful.*

Hillary raises his snow goggles back onto his forehead to see better. He is instantly dazzled by the sun and the swirling crystals of ice. A light breeze blows. He pulls the goggles back down. Eyes watering, he climbs a small depression at the foot of the steep wall. A detour around the wall is impossible. They must somehow climb straight up it. Hillary notices that the ice above him has become separated from the rock, forming a vertical crack. The crevice appears wide enough to climb inside. Before climbing, Hillary takes a photograph of their high-point. With only three and a half hours of oxygen remaining, this summit attempt is a risk. They are too close to turn back now.

There are a few holds on the rocky side of the crack, but the wall of ice on the right side is stable. Hillary addresses

Edmund Hillary at one of the camps on Mount Everest

himself to the rocks and presses one of his crampons into the ice behind him, using bridging techniques. Leaning his oxygen equipment against the ice, he pushes himself upward. Feeling his way from hold to hold, he makes gradual progress. Tensely, nervously, he pushes upward. Finally, he swings safely up onto the upper edge of the twelve-meter step. The last rock step is climbed. Fear and fatigue disappear. With more than 8,800 meters behind them, and only a gently sloping snow ridge ahead, Hillary senses victory.

Tensing Norgay on the summit of Everest

Once his breathing is regular, Hillary gives Tensing the signal to start climbing. Tensing squeezes himself into the chimney while Hillary takes in the rope. Once Tensing reaches Hillary's perch, the two men continue along the ridge. It snakes upward endlessly, each twist and turn concealing the next. The summit seems more out of reach than ever.

Reaching the summit is not just a goal; it is an obsession. Each twist and turn, each setback, makes the craving for success that much keener.

They climb on in an extremely exposed position, perched between the monstrous cornices on the right, which jut out like gigantic balconies over the three-thousand-meter abyss of the Kangshung Face, and the steep rock precipices of the Southwest Face. The endless ridge begins to eat away at their confidence. Then, after an especially steep rise, the vast expanse of Tibet stretches out before them. The ridge with the sweeping cornices drops away to the east. In the distance the pastel-colored hills of the high country of Tibet are barely visible through the thick haze.

The talk of the unconquerable and the unattainable target is stilled. I wondered if ascending Everest would become routine? Will my legend?

The knife-edge of a snow dome to their right is the highest point, the summit of all summits. Using his ice ax, Hillary checks to see if he is standing on a cornice. It is solid. He waves Tensing up and soon both are standing on the Roof of the World.

After fifteen minutes on the summit the two men turn to go. They need only an hour to get back to the South Summit, and by 2 P.M. they have reached the camp on the ridge. Tensing lights the stove and makes some tea. Just before they reach the South Col camp, their oxygen reserves run out.

5.30.1953

The next day at Camp IV is a celebration, filled with shouts of joy and congratulations. Hunt, the expedition leader, blushes as he hugs the "victorious pair."

The successful trio of Hillary, Hunt, and Tensing return to civilization

Hillary and Tenzing fall first into the arms of their comrades and then those of the whole of humanity.

But more and more frequently their talk turns to me and my disappearance. My legend survives their success. It almost seems some believe my ascent was of greater significance than their return.

CHAPTER SEVEN

1960: ORACLE AT MIDNIGHT

The summit of Everest from the north: the last snow slopes and the summit cornice

Do we not destroy something when we need all these men and materials to conquer Everest?

—R. L. G. Irvine

I am awake and I see clearly before me the labyrinth into which they have strayed: too many people and too much money.

—Arnolt Bronnen

IN 1960 THE CHINESE decide to ascend Everest for the
first time. More than twenty trucks bring the expedition team
and equipment to Rongbuk, where a "Himalaya village" is
established. Complete with a clinic, electricity generator, and
radio shack, this village, the highest human settlement in the
world, can accommodate four hundred people. Sayings like
"man will be victorious over nature" and "heroes will climb
up into the skies" are written on the mountain slopes in letters formed from stones.

3.25.1960
More than sixty men, porters and climbers, establish Camp I
on the East Rongbuk Glacier.

3.27.1960
Camp III is established at the foot of the snow slopes below
the North Col, a sight that greatly impresses the Chinese
mountaineers.

*Climbers and a column of porters at the start of the steep slopes
leading to the North Col*

The route is prepared as in the earlier days, but then made
safe with bridges, ladders, and fixed ropes. Camps IV, V, and
Camp VI, at an altitude of 8,100 meters, are established. Two
men manage to reach a height of 8,600 meters, but tragically
two scientists die.

5.4.1960
An unidentifiable corpse is found on the glacier. An old oxygen cylinder, not quite empty, is discovered near Camp V.

136

5.17.1960

Provisions and equipment are sent ahead for the summit team. The porters carry thirty kilograms each to an altitude of 8,500 meters.

5.24.1960

The summit team, consisting of Wang Fuzhou—the leader—Liu Lianman, Qu Yinhua, and the Sherpa Gonbu reach Camp VII. They proceed directly for the summit. It takes five hours—much too long—to climb the Second Step, using up all their pitons. But they press on, climbing onto each other's shoulders to propel them higher. They have still not reached the summit by nightfall.

5.25.1960

In 1953, Hillary and Tensing found no evidence that Mallory and Irvine had been on the summit; the Chinese climbers also do not find any proof that the British pair have been there before them. Thus, the Chinese maintain that they are the first to climb the North Flank, and the first to do so at night.

Later that year the People's Republic of China announces that Everest has been climbed by three Chinese mountaineers via the North Col–North Ridge–Northeast Ridge route on May 25, 1960, at 4:20 A.M. Peking time (2:20 local time). Wang Fuzhou, Qu Yinhua, and Gonbu are said to have been at the summit together. There are no photographs and the published reports are vague. The team is also said to have left a bust of Mao Tse-tung at the top, but no subsequent climbers will ever find a trace of the Mao sculpture.

In pursuit of glory, so many will resort to deceit. The climb should be a personal challenge, not something with which to impress others or to prove one's patriotism.

The Chinese maintain that a successful ascent of Mount Everest was made from the north, despite their lack of proof. Western experts continue to doubt the veracity of their claim.

10.8.1962

A film of the Chinese ascent shown in London is closely scrutinized. By comparing the film with earlier images, experts reveal that the Chinese were actually *below* the Second Step. Unofficially, the Chinese government is forced to admit failure.

Later, the Chinese announce that during the disputed 1960 ascent the climbers found a stick, a piece of rope, and two oxygen bottles above the Second Step.

Given that between 1924 and 1960, only Mallory and Irvine could have climbed beyond the Second Step, this seems to be evidence that one or perhaps both of them had either climbed or detoured around this difficult step.

Which is more honorable: death or failure? To many, I simply died a failure. To others it is my failure that makes me heroic.

Does the "find" made by the Chinese solve the riddle of Mallory and Irvine? Unfortunately, the answer is no. The items are conveniently unavailable. Yet another unfortunate deception.

Nothing was left above the Second Step. But the rubbish left below remains.

CHAPTER EIGHT

1975: TELEPHONES AND HUMAN CHAINS

A column of porters en route for the North Col, 1975

Nine Chinese mountaineers have again conquered the ~~Highest Peak on Earth~~ via the North Face Route and written a new chapter in the history of mountaineering. This deed demonstrates the heroism of the Chinese people, for whom there are no unattainable heights and no fortress that cannot be captured. Of particular importance is the first ascent of the north side of Qomolungma by a female Chinese mountaineer. This represents conclusive proof of what Chairman Mao says: "The times have changed; today men and woman are equal. Whatever a man might achieve, a woman can also do."

—OFFICIAL CHINESE EXPEDITION REPORT

Every poisonous whiff of this land, all the fever and pain suck the lifeblood from me. My dreams are dreams of Death. My morning climbs dizzy ladders to exhaustion. In between, I go to pieces, screaming for peace and time.

—ARNOLT BRONNEN

DURING A RECONNAISSANCE expedition in 1974, the Chinese high-altitude porter Wang Kow Po sees a dead body high up on the North Flank of Mount Everest. It is lying at a height of more than 8,000 meters and in a direct fall-line from the point at which Wyn Harris found the ice ax in 1933. Wang's party wants nothing whatsoever to do with it, and not until years later, when Wang reports his discovery to the Japanese Ryoten Hasegawa, is the find taken seriously.

On October 12, 1979, the day after Wang Kow Po divulged his secret, he is hit by an avalanche below the North Col of Mount Everest, swept into a crevasse, and killed.

In 1975, Wang Fuzhou, one of the Chinese members of the 1960 summit team, is accorded the honor of leader of the Party Committee for the Organization of Everest Expeditions. In the official documents Everest is referred to as *Qomolungma Feng*. This time, in addition to the numerous published reports, a highly impressive documentary film is made of the 1975 Chinese expedition's progress right up to the summit. It is shown at the Trento Mountain Film Festival in 1976.

. . . to tumultuous applause! This time I really have no doubts to voice. I do not want to make myself seen as ridiculous as my countrymen Haston and Scott who in 1975 took photographs of the aluminum tripod left by the Chinese on the summit, to convince the many critics at home that the Chinese had indeed got there before them.

The first Chinese climbers conquered Mount Everest in May 1975, the first English climbers four months later, after the monsoon season. Hillary—despite being known as Sir Edmund Hillary—was and remains a New Zealander, and Tensing Norgay, a Sherpa from Darjeeling. It is true the Sherpa people did originate from Tibet and Tibet was occupied by China, but the People's Republic was too young and too proud to think of Tensing as one of their own. Reason enough to attack Qomolungma Feng with their aluminum ladders.

The expedition takes its leave of Lhasa. A mass celebration marks the occasion. On the big market square beneath the Potala, dancers perform in traditional Tibetan costume while young people wave flags and small children release balloons into the air. A long column of trucks takes the expedition team toward the Himalaya, following a broad, specially widened and asphalted road. There follow some six hundred miles of dusty tracks, taking them through rivers and across

Tibetans and Chinese on the climb to the North Col

scree, before Base Camp is established at 5,000 meters near the Rongbuk Monastery ruins, footage of which is cut from the film.

With a dozen large tents pitched on either side of a wide camp road, Base Camp looks like a military installation—an army camp big enough to hold a battalion. There is even a parade ground equipped with a public-address system and a stage. Everything smacks of military, or rather paramilitary, leadership. Each morning the members of the expedition gather to perform exercises to music. Discipline and order are of paramount importance—there are roll calls, flag parades, orders of the day, staff meetings, and almost daily addresses to the troops.

As Wang Fuzhou later explains, they are under huge pressure to succeed. The soldiers used to form the transport columns beyond Advanced Base are not interested in a cushy assignment—they are members of the elite Red Army Guard. A telephone line is laid between Base Camp and Camp III, together with a path of sorts. Even the route of ascent to the North Col—seamed with crevasses and prone to avalanches—is reconnoitered by special forces, consisting of young climbers and their trainers. The way ahead is prepared with fixed ropes and ladders. Wang recalls that "a group of soldiers and Tibetans, led by the trainers, climbed up to the North Col five times in six days" to stock Camp IV with all the necessary equipment, including hundreds of bottles of oxygen. This was a kind of third base camp, and the point of departure for the climb up to the North Ridge.

4.24.1975

The first assault attempt is aborted due to prolonged high winds. A second attempt on May 8 also fails. Thirty-three climbers in two groups reach Camp VI at 8,200 meters. After thirteen days on the mountain the physical strength of the team is exhausted. They are ordered back to Base Camp. There they decide to resite Camp VI one hundred meters higher, at 8,300 meters. Another camp, Camp VII, is established at 8,600 meters.

5.17.1975

Two groups set off from Base Camp: three women and fifteen men. They are designated the "victory team." The leaders are twenty-nine-year-old Sodnam Norbu and Phantog, a thirty-seven-year-old woman with three children who is also deputy leader of the entire expedition. Both are Tibetan. Team spirit soars. Party officials and a military support unit accompany the team up the mountain.

5.25.1975

They arrive at Camp VI, where two women and seven men have to give up due to exhaustion. Four men reach Camp VII.

5.26.1975

Toward midday, after a stormy night, the weather finally clears and the leadership, or group committee, orders part of the team on ahead to prepare the next section of the route. Fixed ropes are attached to the steep sections of ice and vertical rock

pitches leading up to the Northeast Ridge. Working on two
consecutive days, Sodnam Norbu and Kunga Pasang manage
to fix the Second Step with ropes and a four-section aluminum ladder.

The remaining members of the group, who have been
waiting down at Camp VI, move up to the summit camp,
which is 360 meters high. The climbers avoid most of the ridge
leading to the Second Step by means of a detour onto the
North Flank. At 11 P.M., after a long discussion, the decision is
taken: all nine are to head for the summit the following day.

5.27.1975

By 8 A.M. the nine summit aspirants have left their bivouac in
two groups. The first rope consists of Sodnam Norbu, Darphuntso, Tsering Tobgyal, and Kunga Pasang; the second is
made up of Phantog, Lotse, Hon Sheng-fu, Samdrub, and
Ngapo Khyen. It is still dark and the team soon reaches difficult ground. Progress is slow.

Led by Sodnam Norbu, they climb a six- to seven-meter
high snow step, then the Second Step lies before them. The
climbers grind to a halt at a steep cliff. This is the Second
Step, twenty meters high. The final six meters are nearly
vertical. This section of the route is described in the foreign
literature as an "unclimbable obstacle." The Chinese successfully bypass it on the right. The members of the team belay
each other and ascend the metal ladder anchored in place
by Sodnam Norbu the previous day. But the ladder is not
long enough and a nylon rope is used to replace the missing
rungs right at the top. Leaning back and holding on to the

rope, they pull themselves up. By 9:30 A.M. the Second Step is overcome.

It takes them forty-five minutes to climb the most difficult section. At that height nobody is capable of continuous climbing without a rest.

Ice slopes, scree, and rubble follow. Each step is an eternity. The hours of climbing in the thin air have exhausted the summit assault team. They frequently take short rests and breathe oxygen from the bottles.

The climbers are now about two hundred meters below the summit. The successful conclusion of their task, entrusted to them by the Party and the people, is within reach. And they have made their solemn vows: "As long as the summit remains unclimbed, we will not return!" and "Better to meet with death on the next step forward than to take only half a step backward."

Between the summit and the bivouac at 8,600 meters is a distance of barely a quarter of a mile. But because of the lack of oxygen, the climbers must stop after every step, lean heavily on their ice axes, and take deep breaths.

During the rest stops they inhale bottled oxygen for two or three minutes. Then they take their masks off again. It seems to be helping. Conditions are good. Sixty meters below the summit they make a detour around a steeper ice slope by a traverse to the north, then turn a rock step. One of the team members lapses briefly into unconsciousness, but an oxygen hit revives him.

The summit is reached at 2:30 P.M. with shouts of joy. They ram a ten-foot-high aluminum survey tripod into the snow and raise the Chinese flag. They take photographs, film, and collect samples of rock, ice, and snow. Phantog has to lie flat on the summit for seven minutes while electrocardiograph readings are taken. The team spends seventy minutes on the summit. There is hardly a breath of wind.

5.29.1975

Everyone is back at Base Camp again. The "summit victory" can now be celebrated. The summit team—Phantog, Sodnam Norbu, Lotse, Samdrub, Darphuntso, Kunga Pasang, Tsering Tobgyal, Ngapo Khyen, and the only Chinese member, Hon Sheng-fu, are given the highest awards the state can confer. Now there can be no doubt about it—the north side of Everest has been ascended for the first time.

> *How and where exactly the Chinese failed on the Second Step in 1960 is one thing, how they mastered it in 1975 is another entirely. In any case, without the aluminum ladder, nobody would have succeeded in 1975.*
>
> *It would be tiresome of me to go on about my hobnailed boots again but few could make it as far as the last step wearing something like that. I wonder how the ladder got up there and how it was anchored at the top.*
>
> *Just to get up that high is strenuous work. And to do it while carrying metal ladders on your back, each section a body's length, seems unimaginable. Attaching fixed ropes when climbing the route as a leader is difficult enough. Attaching a ladder to a vertical rock wall demands respect. Of*

*course there were a large number of Chinese—434 in all—
a human chain to the summit. And the Tibetans are skilled
mountaineers, Sodnam Norbu in particular. Nevertheless this
ladder was and remains the key to success. A human pyramid
would not have made it possible to push the route up there.*

*To whom am I saying this? Andrew and I could have
mastered that technology—there were two of us—but aluminum ladders? No. With so much extra weight we would
not even have reached the Second Step.*

*The ladder remains the symbol of the Chinese ascent on
Mount Everest: a collective thing carried up collectively. In
the China of today man conquers nature by sacrificing its
people to the greater good. So many uncomplainingly com-
mit themselves to a greater cause.*

*I do not want to deny the Chinese their share of the suc-
cess; there were hundreds of them on the mountain, but it
was almost exclusively Tibetans who made it to the top.
And what moves me about these Tibetans, fills me with
such admiration, is above all their humanity, compassion,
commitment, their tolerance toward the Chinese, who even
during this ascent were guilty of denigrating the Tibetan cul-
ture.*

When finally they reach the summit, the Chinese and Ti-
betans are still some way from being on equal footing. The
Party leadership in Peking only recognizes the success of
Communism. This is the only newsworthy item.

The official report of the climb announces a "great victory":

151

On 27 May 1975 nine Chinese mountaineers, one woman and eight men, their resolve strengthened by the active participation of Chairman Mao and the Central Committee of the Communist Party of China and with the warmhearted support of the people of the whole country, made a victorious ascent of Qomolungma via the North Face. It was a great victory of Chairman Mao's proletarian revolutionary line, the fruitful achievement of the great Proletarian Cultural Revolution.

China seems to be fostering the development of climbing as a sport that serves the ideals of proletarian politics and national defense strategies, while at the same time helps the people toward the goal of physical strength and discipline, that they might fear neither adversity nor death, and thus serve the greater good of the collective with body and soul.

I find it all so difficult. My mountain as a symbol for Communist ideals? Nonsense. Yet that seems to be what it is all coming to. I do not consider my death tragic. Tragedy is the death of the soul, not the body.

The Chinese had their ladder. I had my spirit.

CHAPTER NINE

1924: THE LAST CLIMB

The ascent to the North Col

On 6 June 1924 we said good-bye to Mallory and Irvine forever. The last gesture was a handshake and a blessing. I saw no more of them.

—EDWARD FELIX NORTON

BY THE TIME I solo-climbed Mount Everest in 1980, there had been fifty-six summit attempts. Most were successful. And yet, none of those climbs, including my own, match what Mallory and Irvine did in June 1924. Mallory who gave the mountain a spirit that cannot be captured with radio or telephone equipment, nor seen with telephoto lenses or satellite pictures. Daring to attempt the impossible, risking everything for a dream, and refusing to capitulate in the face of adversity, Mallory, to me, personifies heroism.

There is limited information about Mallory and Irvine's last climb and no written record of their final days other than a few notes from Mallory and a few journal entries by Odell. Yet, Mallory more than anyone else gives a historical dimension to Mount Everest. Using my knowledge of the terrain and of Mallory, I've tried to re-create their last moments. It is impossible to know what really happened. But if Mallory taught me anything, it is that we cannot accept the impossible and must learn to celebrate the possible.

The north side of Everest, 1924

1. Camp VI at 8,140 meters

2. Somervell's 1924 high-point

3. Norton's 1924 high-point

4. The Second Step: last sighting of Mallory and Irvine

5. First Step

6. The point reached by Finch and Geoffrey Bruce in 1922

7. The point reached by Mallory, Norton, and Somervell in 1922

8. The summit of Mount Everest at 8,848 meters

Following the attempts to scale Mount Everest in 1921 and 1922, Mallory prepares for one last attempt in 1924. This time he opted to go with Andrew Irvine—and with oxygen. There were enough porters, and the weather was fine. The tents at Camps V and VI were still available, and the Sherpas would carry the oxygen bottles.

Norton did not agree with Mallory's choice of Irvine as his companion, but said nothing. Irvine was suffering from a sore throat and had little mountaineering experience. Odell was in better shape and would have seemed the better choice. But Mallory was adamant about climbing with Irvine.

> *I wanted Irvine because of his competence with the oxygen equipment, his intuitive grasp of technical matters, his enthusiasm, and his cheerful camaraderie. These made him the ideal partner. His alpine experience was limited to rock climbing on British mountains and a few mountain climbs in Spitsbergen, but I had great confidence in his mental and physical skills.*

6.5.1924

Mallory and Irvine make their final preparations. Eight porters, fresh and well rested, are to take the loads up to Camp VI. Despite being snow-blind, Norton, who speaks Nepali, visits the porters' tent from time to time to build up their courage. Hazard and Odell decide to stay at the North Col.

6.6.1924

Hazard and Odell bring breakfast to the two aspiring summiteers. While Norton is half-led, half-carried down to Camp

Edward Norton below the summit of Everest, 1924

III, Mallory and Irvine reach Camp V. Four of the eight porters are so debilitated they must turn back. On a scrap of paper, Mallory writes a message to Odell: "There is no wind up here and things look hopeful." At 5 P.M. the four porters return to Odell with Mallory's message.

6.7.1924

Norton remains at Camp III with Bruce, Noel, and Hingston to await the return of the summit party. At Camp V, Mallory and Irvine begin the climb to Camp VI. Later in the afternoon, Odell arrives at Camp V with one porter. He is greeted by the four remaining porters in Mallory's team. They have a letter from Mallory:

Dear Odell,

We're awfully sorry to have left things in such a mess—our Unna Cooker rolled down the slope at the last moment. Be sure of getting back to IV tomorrow to evacuate before dark, as I hope to. In the tent I must have left a compass—for the Lord's sake rescue it: we are here without. To here on 90 atmospheres for the two days—so we'll probably go on two cylinders—but it's a bloody load for climbing. Perfect weather for the job!

Yours ever,

George Mallory

Odell's porter is ill and goes back down with the others. Odell remains at Camp V alone and muses on the phenomenon of altitude sickness:

> It is wonderful how that strange malady, so often described as "mountain sickness," seems to disappear not only with the descent, but when a decision to descend has been made: at any rate I have noticed it time and again with these native porters, if not with other climbers! When no further effort is to be called for, the psychological effect is such that a fresh stimulus to normality is given, and sickness and other effects disappear.

The day ends, and the fading light lends the surrounding mountains a violet glow. Far below, the glaciers look like streams of gray vapor. Odell has never experienced silence like this before.

> *Higher up, we crouched in the tent and I melted ice continuously while Andrew tinkered with the oxygen apparatus. This technology was our only hope. Our worries, plus the altitude headaches and the rapid breathing, prevented us from dozing off. Once again the new day dispels any gloomy feelings of defeat and we are again inspired by that distant point—the greatest of heights.*

6.8.1924

The morning is calm and not particularly cold: time to set off from Camp VI. Mallory heads off toward the Northeast

Ridge, and Irvine follows. Both use the oxygen systems that Irvine has repaired. Negotiating steep rock sections and scrambling over ledge systems, moving more slowly than they'd expected to, they reach easier terrain and traverse beneath the First Step on its north side below the ridge, making for the summit. They do not actually climb the First Step but keep to the ledges below the crest of the ridge. Once or twice they wander onto the ridge itself and are then visible from below, silhouetted against the sky.

Odell has a trouble-free sleep. In the morning he climbs up the slopes above Camp V. Later, he recalls the situation exactly:

> Carrying a rucksack with provisions in case of shortage at Camp VI, I made my solitary way up the steep slope of snow and rock behind Camp V and so reached the crest of the main North Ridge. The earlier morning had been clear and not unduly cold, but now rolling banks of mist commenced to form and sweep from the westward across the great face of the mountain. But it was fortunate that the wind did not increase. There were indications though that this mist might be chiefly confined to the lower half of the mountain, as on looking up one could see a certain luminosity that might mean comparatively clear conditions about its upper half. This appearance so impressed me that I had no qualms for Mallory and Irvine's progress upward from Camp VI, and I hoped by this time that they would be well on their way up

the final pyramid of the summit. The wind being light, they should have made good progress and un-hampered by their intended route along the crest of the north-east shoulder.

Anyone who has set off three times to climb Mount Everest as I had would not sit around in the final camp when good weather prevails. Little matter that during the night every-thing in the tent had frozen stiff—the ropes and the hob-nailed boots, the valves on the oxygen apparatus and the cooker. Once outside the tent and on your feet there is only one way to go—onward.

The monsoon fog swirled around the slopes beneath us, but on the ridge it was clear. We left camp VI a little late and our progress was slow. Beneath the ridge were ledges with rock slabs in layers sloping downward, and on the summit ridge were humps that we could not avoid. We climbed and rested and looked around. The horizons were so far away and our tortured bodies could find no safe place to rest. The tent was still there but could no longer be seen. It lay far be-hind us as a last bastion of calm and security. Ahead of us, in the bright light, like a column towering into the sky, was the summit, signifying greatness.

As Odell approaches 8,000 meters, the mist clears.

[T]here was a sudden clearing of the atmosphere above me and I saw the whole summit ridge and final peak of Everest unveiled. I noticed far away on a snow slope

162

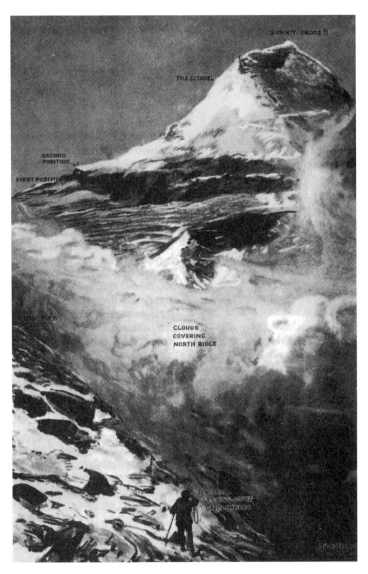

Odell's last view of Mallory and Irvine's ascent

THE SECOND DEATH OF GEORGE MALLORY

leading up to what seemed to me to be the last step but one from the base of the final pyramid, a tiny object moving and approaching the rock step. A second object followed, and then the first climbed to the top of the step. As I stood intently watching this dramatic appearance, the scene became enveloped in cloud once more, and I could not actually be certain that I saw the second figure join the first. It was of course none other than Mallory and Irvine, and I was surprised above all to see them so late as this, namely 12:50, at a point which, if the "second rock step," they should have reached according to Mallory's schedule by 8 A.M. at the latest, and if the "first rock step" proportionately earlier. The "second rock step" is seen prominently in photographs of the North Face from the Base Camp, where it appears a short distance from the base of the final pyramid down the snowy first part of the crest of the North-east Arête. The lower "first rock step" is about an equivalent distance again to the left. Owing to the small portion of the summit ridge uncovered I could not be precisely certain at which of these two "steps" they were, as in profile and from below they are very similar, but at the time I took it for the upper "second step." However, I am a little doubtful now whether the latter would not be hidden by the projecting nearer ground from my position below on the face. I could see that they were moving expeditiously as if endeavouring to make up for lost time.

Noel Odell was a brilliant geologist. He was also well acclimatized, tenacious, and skillful. Nevertheless, he remains a questionable witness. He told his story often and each time somewhat differently. One wonders how much of his sighting of Mallory and Irvine can be attributed to hope and guilt. At any rate, because of the late hour and difficult terrain, the two men were probably between the First and Second Steps when Odell saw them.

Odell might have been able to see us on the First Step or above the Second Step through a hole in the cloud, but I could not see him. From this distance it is only possible to make out a person if he is a silhouette against the sky; otherwise, he would be lost against the dark scree slopes of the north face.

At 12:50 the mist descends between the ridge and Odell. "Why are they still only there?" he asks himself. They had intended to reach the Second Step by about 8 A.M. He wonders what could have delayed them.

True, they were moving one at a time over what was apparently but moderately difficult ground, but one cannot definitely conclude from this that they were roped together—a not unimportant consideration in any estimate of what may eventually have befallen them. I had seen that there was a considerable quantity of new snow covering some of the upper rocks near the summit ridge, and this may well have caused delay in the ascent. Burdened as they undoubtedly would have been with the oxygen apparatus, these snow-covered debris-sprinkled slabs may have given much trouble. The oxygen apparatus itself may have needed repair or readjustment either before or after they left Camp VI, and so have delayed them. Though rather unlikely, it is just conceivable that the zone of mist and clouds I had experienced below may have extended up to their level and so have somewhat impeded their progress.

In spite of the late hour Mallory urges Irvine on. Now that the summit is so close, his determination grows. Crystals of ice whip through the air, and the clouds boil high above the Kharta Valley. When the clouds part for a moment, the bright sunlight dazzles them. They now must wear their snow goggles—a kind of welder's glasses with dark, round lenses and leather-covered frames.

Suddenly they see a huge rock step towering over them, its size grotesquely magnified by the swirling veils of mist. Rising in two distinct sweeps, it blocks the way. Scaling it is impossible—it is far too high, too smooth, too exposed. One false step and they would be killed. And without any place to anchor it, the rope is useless here. Mallory risks a look at the arête on the left: unthinkable. A bottomless abyss yawns beneath him. To the right, an insurmountable belt of rocks bars the way. It is impossible to climb any farther.

It was obvious: We had to turn back. Back, I said to myself,
always back. We can only save ourselves by descending.
I wondered how I was to come to terms with yet another
failure.

When Odell reaches Camp VI at 2 P.M., it begins to snow.
The wind rises. He places some provisions in the tent and has
a look around. Inside the tent, articles of clothing, food, oxygen bottles, and pieces of apparatus are strewn everywhere.
Outside he sees oxygen sets and the duralumim frames onto
which are lashed the steel canisters. It looks as if Mallory and
Irvine have been working on the apparatus. Odell suspects
they are having difficulty with the equipment.

Odell can find no note, no message. When did the two men
set off then? He knows that in the mist and in this weather the
camp between the rocks would not be easy to find, so he
climbs about sixty meters farther up, toward the summit. He
can only see a few meters ahead. He whistles and shouts in case
they are within earshot. He moves behind a boulder to take
shelter from the windblown snow and crouches there for a
while.

When Odell gets back to Camp VI, the storm has abated.
The sun is shining and the light new snow evaporates without
melting. For a brief moment the summit region becomes visible. There is no sign of the two climbers.

There is only room for two men in the tent, and Odell re-
members that Mallory expressly requested that Odell descend
to the North Col in good time. So at 4:30 P.M. he leaves the

camp, still without having seen anyone. He descends quickly. Between 7,560 and 7,160 meters the snow is hard and the terrain steep enough for a swift glissade. He is back at the North Col by 6:45 P.M. He manages the return trip from Camp V to Camp IV in just thirty-five minutes and notes that he finds the descent only marginally more demanding than it would be at a more modest altitude:

> It was interesting to find, as I had earlier, that descending at high altitudes is little more fatiguing than at any other moderate altitudes, and of course in complete contrast to the extraordinarily exhausting reverse of it, and it seemed that a party that has not completely shot its bolt and run itself to a standstill, so to speak, on the ascent, and in any attempt on the summit, should find itself unexpectedly able to make fast time downward and escape being benighted. And as I shall mention later, the unnecessity of oxygen for the properly acclimatized climber seems never more evident than in this capability of quick descent.

Odell arrives back at Camp IV dehydrated, and Hazard brings him tea and soup, to replace the liquids he has lost over the last two days.

Have Mallory and Irvine reached Camp VI or V meanwhile? As darkness falls, Odell and Hazard step out of the tent once more to look for signs of life on the summit. All they can see is the outline of the mountain.

. . .

Having failed to surmount the Second Step, Mallory and Irvine begin their descent. It is much later than they had thought: Night is falling quickly. Their descent is made even more dangerous by a brewing snowstorm. Mallory carefully leads them past the First Step. As it gets darker and the intensity of the storm increases, they became desperate to make it back to camp. They do not even want to stop to signal for help. They know that in these conditions no one survives unprotected. Their oxygen runs out. They discard the heavy apparatus and keep going. Lethargy forces them to stop after every step, and they have difficulty finding secure footholds for their heavy, nailed boots. The circumstances are ripe for an accident.

All the horrors of hell converged beneath the summit. We were far too slow. There was the darkness, the route long since lost in the whiteout. There was hardly anything to aid one's sense of direction in the fading light—just yawning depths everywhere. And that dead air! Even the firmament had become a gaping abyss. Suddenly everything became uncertain: the rescue, the next step, my partner on the rope. We experienced something deeper than despair as we felt our way through our terrors, and then—a sudden jerk—the release, the fall.

CHAPTER TEN

1999: HOBNAILED BOOTS AND THE INTERNET

Mallory at Base Camp in 1922

For Mallory, reaching the summit meant the realization of his life's ambition. The mountain had become a fixed idea for him and he had to make this idea a reality, at any price. He had no other ties other than those that bound him to Everest; everything else had been left behind. When he stood on the top the mountain and he would become one.

—WALTER BAUER

IMMEDIATELY FOLLOWING MALLORY'S death came an age of setting records. What counted was being the first or the fastest or the highest. We still live in that age, though to some degree it has passed Mount Everest by, or turned what had been a symbol of the impossible into a mere matter of the affordable. Scaling Mount Everest has now become the ultimate extreme vacation for adventure seekers. Tour operators and professional guides, more concerned with profit than with safety, have turned a spiritual quest into a cold-blooded accomplishment. To paraphrase Oscar Wilde's definition of a cynic, everyone knows the price of the highest peak in the world, and no one knows its value. In 1996 some Indian climbers were dangling on the summit ridge, nor far from the Second Step. A Japanese group climbed past the dying men, ignoring their pleas for help. The Japanese wanted to get to the summit; they were in a hurry. The motto of a whole generation of climbers is no longer what it was in Mallory's day—to complete one task well—but to do as many things as possible simultaneously, and then to immediately move on to the next. Under these circumstances, what can the modern climber understand of the danger and uncertainty of route-finding?

Mallory's body remained hidden for seventy-five years. Many climbing expeditions, fixated on reaching the summit, trooped past him. Only in the spring of 1999, with twenty-two teams attempting to climb Everest from the north, fourteen groups at work on the south side, and one trying the eastern approach, was his body found.

5.1.1999

About midday, a member of the Mallory & Irvine Research Expedition on Mount Everest, Conrad Anker, notices a "strange patch of white" on a ledge at 8,250 meters. Shortly afterwards he is looking at a wax-white corpse, whose clothing disintegrates upon touch. On the left foot is a well-preserved hobnailed boot. The shin and calf bones appear to be broken. When they find the initials G.L.M. stitched into a handkerchief and shirt collar and a letter written by Ruth Mallory in a side pocket, the identity of the body is clear.

It lies on a terrace twenty meters below the Northeast Ridge and about 230 meters east of the First Step. It was in this area in 1933 that Wyn Harris discovered an ice ax thought to belong to Irvine. "When we realized that this was Mallory, we were fascinated," climber Dave Hahn later explained. "We did not want to disturb him; after all, he had been lying there for seventy-five years. But at the same time we thought we could do him no better honor than to find out if he had reached the summit in 1924."

The climbing team, made up of six American climbers in addition to the leader Eric Simonson, the German Jochen Hemmleb, and a British climber, are both delighted and awed by their discovery. "The team performed a committal ceremony and then buried George Mallory," Simonson reports via the Internet.

"Our work is not finished, this is just the start," Simonson later announced. The team has been on the go since March 29 and is battling acute fatigue and stress. "You take one step and you do not think about George Mallory anymore, you are concerned for your own life because you could fall," admitted Dave Hahn after the ceremony.

How can the expedition members determine whether Mallory and Irvine climbed the highest mountain on earth twenty-nine years before Edmund Hillary and Tensing Norgay? They hope to find the little pocket camera with which the two Englishmen could have taken photos of the summit. Experts believe that the film might still be developed if no light has penetrated the camera.

5.13.1999

Simonson's expedition rescues a Ukranian climber and then rests for the remainder of the day. They must prepare for their own summit attempt. A strong team from the Research Expedition is already on its way to Camp V.

5.15.1999

Hurricane-force winds howl across Mount Everest. The team spends another night at Camp V. Slowly, the weather improves.

5.17.1999

Summit day.

The assault team is up at midnight and starts climbing shortly after 2 A.M. New snow blankets the ledges and a plume of snow blows from the summit. It is very cold. By 9 A.M. the weather is clear and the sun provides much-needed warmth. Dave Hahn and Conrad Anker are past the First Step. At the start of the traverse to the Second Step, where the Chinese established their Camp VII in 1975, Hahn and Anker take a breather. Even for them, taking the direct route up the ridge is out of the question—the arête *is* simply unclimbable. "It is not only unlikely that Mallory climbed this Step 'free,'" Anker thinks, "it is impossible."

The climbers follow the traditional route on the north side of the ridge, skirting the Second Step by climbing rock steps and a ramp on the right. Despite the intense cold Anker wants to climb the crux free, without the ladders and fixed ropes used by previous climbers.

Hahn and Anker traverse farther across the ridge to the Second Step and work their way up the first few rock steps. Anker manages to "free climb" the Second Step. A wide crack to the left of the ladder placed by the Chinese in 1975 provides assistance. Though choked with snow it is not an easy climb. Hanging over it is a wedge of rock barring the way up. Anker makes a daring bridging move across to the fixed ropes and continues in an arc up until he finally reaches the flat capping roof above the exposed passage. At an altitude of 8,600 meters, this is an extraordinary achievement.

Anker has left his rucksack with his oxygen apparatus at the bottom of the crux pitch to improve his chances of climbing it. Hahn comes up on the ladder, bringing Anker's rucksack up with him. The route from the top of the Second Step to the summit is well marked, but strenuous. Meanwhile, the rest of the team goes down to Camp VI.

The long haul to the top and the worsening weather take their toll on Anker and Hahn. It takes them four hours to get from the Second Step to the summit. Eventually they make it to the top. One hundred and seventeen other climbers, male and female, have scaled Mount Everest in the 1999 pre-monsoon season. Forty-eight of them came from the north, sixty-six from the south, three from the eastern side of the mountain. For forty-seven of them, this was not even the first time they had stood on the top of the world.

It is snowing hard as Hahn and Anker begin the descent to camp. There is a whiteout and the two men have a long way to go. Proceeding slowly and carefully, they eventually make it back and take their place in the record books as the men who established six new meters of free-climbing on Mount Everest.

The Second Step consists of only three meters of rock, and yet it is one of the most treacherous areas on Everest. I have no doubt that Mallory realized this. I wonder if his disap-pointment didn't destroy his confidence and drain his last reserve of strength. Having exhausted every possibility, and with his oxygen gone, he turned, started back down, and lost his way in the mist.

Today, no one on the route is ever as isolated and alone as Mallory was in June 1924. Thanks to helicopters, telephones, fax machines, and the Internet, climbers on Mount Everest are constantly connected to the world. Rather than trekking up, people even fly straight into Everest Base Camp. With our superlightweight oxygen sets, performance clothing, and high-tech gear, soon nearly anyone will be fit enough for the mountain.

5.17.1999

Anker and Hahn descend. At five o'clock in the afternoon, two climbers go up to meet the summit pair and help them down. They all arrive safely back at Camp VI at 8,300 meters.

5.18.1999

The members of the Mallory & Irvine Research Expedition arrive at Advanced Base Camp. The expedition leader asks that the whole world believe that Mallory and Irvine did reach the summit. Via the Internet, the message is spread.

I note that now I seem to be expected to share my humble resting place on Mount Everest. So be it. They might actually have found me seventy-five years ago. I must say that I am a little relieved that it will be impossible for them to transport me off the mountain and that I will be permitted to remain.

I hasten to add I am by no means alone. Others have fallen where I fell. Dozens of other corpses strew the path to the summit. Some, sadly, were searching for my mortal remains.

I find all the honor heaped upon me somewhat disconcerting and unseemly. When my discoverers emptied my pockets, they were—poor fellows—gasping for breath and clearing their throats. One mistook a black lump of rock in my hands for a Kodak camera. They spoke of "sensation," "unambiguous," and "proof."

How strange to have one's death announced to the world by satellite. Oddly, I have never felt more alone.

Later, they may maintain that they made me a better resting place. One thing seems certain: Finding my body was not the only goal of their expedition. They are after something more difficult to find than hard evidence.

Perhaps if they searched their hearts, they might see that they do not really want to know everything. Some things should remain untouched and unmeasured. There is no further reason to disturb me, Simonson says. But still I wonder, will they truly leave me in peace?

"Well done," I would tell my discoverers. But there was Anker, one of the best all-round mountaineers in the world, secured by a modern piece of equipment that jams itself into rock; above this he can attach himself to fixed points, because there are no natural belays. Could he have managed without modern technology? And I had been so proud of my specially designed hobnailed boots.

When the prospect of going to Mount Everest first opened for me, I used to visualize the expedition in my thoughts as a series of tremendous, panting efforts up the final steps, a challenge to body and soul, and demanding every ounce of perseverance.

My desire to reach the summit grew, over time, into a need to believe in man's capabilities. I gather this spirit inspired modern alpinism. Anyone wanting to reach the summit must lift his spirits to its heights.

AFTERWORD

Reinhold Messner with Captain Noel and Professor Odell in 1982

Mallory descended so that he might return another time. The flame that burned within him had been dampened down. He saw the mountain, but to do so he did not need to raise his eyes, for Everest was within him, it had become the focal point of his life.

—WALTER BAUER

No matter when and how Everest may be climbed, Mallory's name is inseparably associated with the great struggle to win the highest point on earth for those whose idea of possession is limited to what has been trodden on or handled.

—R. L. G. IRVINE

IN FEBRUARY 1982, I MET Captain Noel and Professor Odell in London to discuss the tragic 1924 expedition, particularly the disappearance of Mallory and Irvine. Odell, ninety-one at the time, suspected that Mallory and Irvine had met their fate during the descent from the summit. Odell has said:

> The question remains, "Has Mount Everest been climbed?" It must be left unanswered, for there is no direct evidence. But bearing in mind all the circumstances, and considering their position when last seen, I think myself that there is a strong probability that Mallory and Irvine succeeded.

During our conversation, Odell confirmed that he had seen Mallory and Irvine on June 8, 1924, on the Northeast Ridge. He vividly described how through a chink in the fog, he was able to see them climbing one of the steps on the long, drawn-out ridge. Yet, Odell was still unable to specify exactly which of the many steps. Since this activity was over quickly, taking no longer than five minutes according to Odell, it is obvious to me that Mallory and Irvine could not have been climbing the Second Step. Without a ladder or modern equipment, it would be impossible for them to climb the Second Step that quickly. Even today it would take thirty to sixty minutes. Nor could they have gone around it with the equipment they had available in 1924, neither via the ice- and snow-covered east face, nor via the Norton Couloir. I also know that in 1924, due to lack of time and other difficulties, a summit bid without bivouacking was unthinkable. And a bivouac during the ascent or shortly after the summit would have weakened the mountaineers too much. If they had man-

View up the summit of Everest as seen from the west

1. First Step
2. Second Step
3. Exit of the Grand Couloir
4. Main Summit
5. South Summit (hidden from view)

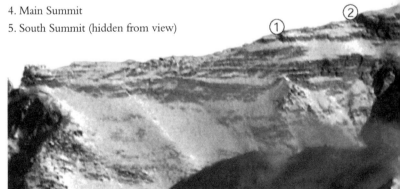

aged to bivouac, they would have died higher up and not where Mallory was found in 1999. Therefore, it is my belief that Odell spotted the pair somewhere in between the First and Second Step and that they turned back at the Second Step only to perish on the descent. As much as I may wish that Mallory and Irvine did reach the summit of Mount Everest in 1924, I accept that all the evidence is against it. The terrain of the summit region, the equipment available in 1924, and the location of the frozen body support the theory that Mallory failed.

Since their discovery, Mallory's physical remains have been marketed extensively. Photographs of the body were immediately available for sale worldwide. Hillary, now eighty-two years old, has become especially dismayed by the profiteering.

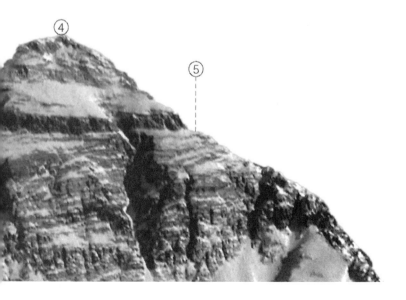

Even though the money will now be donated to a Himalayan charity, the exploitive nature of the project remains.

Nevertheless, Mallory's spirit lives on. In 1995, George Mallory Jr., grandson to George Leigh Mallory, climbed Mount Everest via the North Ridge. A Mallory had at last reached the summit.

NOTES ON SOURCES

Throughout this book, I have tried to remain true to both the spirit and letter of George L. Mallory and his contemporaries and have therefore quoted from works containing their original writings and correspondence—many of which are now out of print and hard to locate. With the combined resources of the Sheffield Libraries, the Alpine Club, and Ken Wilson's excellent archives, I was fortunate enough to find and use the following works:

Bruce, Charles. *The Assault on Mount Everest, 1922*. London: Edward Arnold & Co., 1923. This is a dramatic account of the second British Mount Everest expedition, which followed the route of the reconnaissance expedition of 1921 and reached an altitude of 8,320 meters but then had to turn back.

Finch, George Ingle. *Climbing Mount Everest*. London: G. Philip, 1930.

Howard-Bury, C. K., et al. *Mount Everest: The Reconnaissance, 1921*. London: Hodder & Stoughton, 1921. A comprehensive narrative of the expedition and the reconnaissance of the mountain includes the natural history of the area and copious appendixes covering a survey, photographic survey, geological results, scientific equipment, and mammals, birds, and plants.

Norton, Edward Felix, et al. *The Fight for Everest, 1924.* London: Edward Arnold & Co., 1925. Includes contributions by C. G. Bruce and N. E. Odell among others, as well as Mallory's letters.

Younghusband, Francis. *The Epic of Mount Everest.* London: Edward Arnold & Co., 1926. Written on behalf of the Mount Everest Committee and based on original accounts, this is a condensed description of three expeditions to Everest: the assaults and ascents of 1921, 1922, and 1924.

BIBLIOGRAPHY

Bauer, Walter. *Mount Everest: Bericht von Mallory und seinen Freunden.* Gütersloh: Bertelsmann, 1952.

Bronnen, Arnolt. *Ostpolzug.* In Arnolt Bronnen, *Werke in 5 Bänden.* Edited by Friedbert Aspetsberger. Klagenfurt: Ritter, 1989.

Bruce, Charles G., et al. *Mount Everest: Der Angriff 1922.* Basel: Benno Schwabe, 1924.

Carr, Herbert. *The Irvine Diaries: Andrew Irvine and the Enigma of Everest, 1924.* N. p.: Gastrus-West Col Publications, 1979.

Dyhrenfurth, Günter Oskar. *Der dritte Pol: Die Achttausender und ihre Trabanten.* München: Nymphenburger Verlagshandlung, 1960.

Finch, George Ingle. *Der Kampf um den Everest.* Leipzig: F. A. Brockhaus, 1925.

Flaig, Walther. *Im Kampf um Tschomo-lungma, den Gipfel der Erde.* Stuttgart: Franckh'sche Verlagshandlung, 1923.

Hillary, Edmund. *Ich stand auf dem Everest: Meine Erstbesteigung mit Scherpa Tensing.* Wiesbaden: F. A. Brockhaus, 1974.

Howard-Bury, C. K., et al. *Mount Everest: Die Erkundungsfahrt 1921.* Basel: Benno Schwabe, 1922.

Irvine, R. L. G. *Werden und Wandlungen des Bergsteigens.* Wien: Verlag Adolf Holzhausens Nachf., 1949.

Messner, Reinhold. *Nie zurück.* München: BLV, 1997.

———. *Everest. Expedition zum Endpunkt.* München: BLV, 1998.

N. N. *Erneute Besteigung des höchsten Gipfels der Welt—des Qomolungma.* Peking: Verlag für fremdsprachige Literatur, 1975.

Norton, Edward Felix, et al. *Bis zur Spitze des Mount Everest. Die Besteigung 1924.* Basel: Benno Schwabe, 1926.

Unsworth, Walt. *Everest.* London: Allen Lane/Penguin Books, 1981.

Younghusband, Francis. *Der Himalaja ruft.* Berlin: Union Deutsche Verlagsgesellschaft, n.d.

Zhou Zheng/Liu Zhenkai. *Footprints on the Peaks: Mountaineering in China.* N.p., n.d.

For Further Reading

Aufmuth, Ulrich. "Die Lust am Risiko." *Berg '85, Alpenvereinsjahrbuch* 109 (München, 1984): 87–102.

Bell, S. "Gear Special—Commercial Expeditions." *Mountain* 132 (1990): 43–44.

Boardman, P. *Sacred Summits.* London: Hodder & Stoughton, 1982.

Bonington, Chris. *Everest—the Hard Way.* London: Hodder & Stoughton, 1976.

Braham, T. "The Himalaya—Winds of a Change." *Alpine Journal* 78 (1973): 57–61.

Burgess, A./Palmer, J.: *Everest—the Ultimate Challenge.* London: Hodder & Stoughton, 1983.

Chan-Chun, S. "The Conquest of Mount Everest by the Chinese Mountaineering Team." *Himalayan Journal* 23 (1961): 151–68.

Collister, R. "Small Expeditions in the Himalaya." *Alpine Journal* 84 (1979): 166–72.

———. *Lightweight Expeditions.* Ramsbury: Crowood Press, 1989.

Cullen, R. "Expeditions, Efficiency, Ethics and the Environment." *Leisure Studies* 6 (1987): 41–53.

Deegan, P. "Rescue on Everest." *High* 165 (1996): 86–88.

Denman, E. *Alone to Everest.* London: Collins, 1954.

Dyhrenfurth, N. G./Unsoeld, Willi F. "Mount Everest, 1963." *Himalayan Journal* 25 (1964): 3–31.

Eggler, A. "The Swiss Expedition to Everest and Lhotse." *Himalayan Journal* 20 (1957): 3–10.

Faarlund, N. "Bergsteigen—warum?" *Berg '75, Alpenvereinsjahrbuch* 100 (München, 1974): 141–47.

Faux, R. "Everest NE Ridge—The Seligmann Harris Expedition." *Alpine Journal* 92 (1987): 92–97.

Finch, George Ingle. "The Second Attempt on Everest." *Alpine Journal* 34 (1921/22): 439–52.

Freshfield, Douglas W. "The Conquest of Mount Everest." *Alpine Journal* 36 (1924): 1–11.

Gray, D. "The Himalayan Ethic—Time for Rethink." *Alpine Journal* 76 (1971): 156–61.

Himalayan Club. "The Problem of Mount Everest." *Himalayan Journal* 9 (1937): 111–20 (with a commentary by Eric Shipton, pp. 120–26).

Hoelzel, Tom. "The Chinese 1960 Ascent of Mount Everest." *Mountain* 101 (1985): 39–43.

Houston, C. "Towards Everest, 1950." *Himalayan Journal* 17 (1952): 10–18.

Howard-Bury, C. K. "The 1921 Mount Everest Expedition." *Alpine Journal* 34 (1921/22): 195–214.

Hunt, J. *The Ascent of Everest.* London: Hodder & Stoughton, 1953.

Kohli, M. S. "Nine atop Everest." *Himalayan Journal* 26 (1965): 3–19.

Lester, J. T. "Personality and Everest." *Alpine Journal* 74 (1969): 101–7.

Mallory, George Leigh. "Mount Everest: The Reconnaissance." *Alpine Journal* 34 (1921/22): 215–27.

———. "The Second Mount Everest Expedition." *Alpine Journal* 34 (1921/22): 425–39.

Messner, Reinhold. *Überlebt: Alle 14 Achttausender, mit Chronik,* München: BLV, 1999.

Murray, W. H. "The Reconnaissance of Mount Everest, 1951." *Himalayan Journal* 17 (1952): 19–41.

Norton, Edward Felix. "The Mount Everest Dispatches." *Alpine Journal* 36 (1924): 196–241.

Noyce, Wilfried. *South Col: One Man's Adventure on the Ascent of Everest, 1953.* London: Heinemann, 1954.

Oelz, Oswald. "Tendenzen des Bergsteigens im Himalaja." *Die Alpen/Les Alpes* 64 (1988): 31–40.

Pugh, L. Griffith. "Scientific Problems on Mount Everest." *Himalayan Journal* 23 (1954): 46–58.

Roberts, D. *I'll Climb Mount Everest Alone—the Story of Maurice Wilson.* London: Robert Hale, 1957.

Ruttledge, Hugh. "The Mount Everest Expedition of 1933." *Himalayan Journal* 6 (1933): 31–46.

———. *Everest 1933.* London: Hodder & Stoughton, 1934.

———. "The Mount Everest Expedition of 1936." *Himalayan Journal* 9 (1937): 3–15.

Sayre, W. W. *Four Against Everest.* London: Arthur Barker, 1964.

Scott, Doug. "Northeast Ridge of Everest, 1987 Expedition." *Himalayan Journal* 45 (1987/88): 117–23.

Shipton, Eric. "Everest, 1933—Extracts from the Everest Diary." *Alpine Journal* 46 (1934): 111–18.

———. "The Mount Everest Reconnaissance, 1935." *Himalayan Journal* 8 (1936): 1–13.

Singh, G. "Indians on Mount Everest." *Himalayan Journal* 22 (1959/60): 3–12.

Smythe, Frank S. *Camp Six, An Account of the 1933 Mount Everest Expedition.* London: Hodder & Stoughton, n.d.

———. *Spirit of the Hills.* London: Hodder & Stoughton, 1935.

Styles, S. *On Top of the World.* London: Hamish Hamilton, 1967.

Tasker, Joe. "Small Expeditions." *Alpine Journal* 82 (1977): 21–28.

———. *Everest the Cruel Way.* London: Methuen, 1981.

Tilman, H. William. "Mount Everest, 1938." *Himalayan Journal* 11 (1939): 1–14.

———. *Mount Everest, 1938.* Cambridge: Cambridge University Press, 1948.

Tinker, J. "Climbing the North Ridge of Everest." *Alpine Journal* 100 (1995): 25–36.

Williams, M. "Everest Diary." *Summit* (spring 1991): 8–11.

INDEX

Note: Page references to photographs are in italics.

ABOUT THE AUTHOR

Reinhold Messner was introduced to mountaineering by his father, and from the age of thirteen he made numerous difficult climbs in the Eastern Alps. In 1970 he scaled Nanga Parbat I (26,660 feet [8,126 m]) in the Himalayas by way of its Rupal (south) face; his younger brother Günther died during the descent. In 1975, Messner and Peter Habeler of Austria made the first ascent of the northwestern face of Gasherbrum I (Hidden Peak; 26,470 feet [8,068 m]) in the Karakoram Range, without oxygen or support climbers. In 1978, Messner again climbed Nanga Parbat I, reaching the summit alone by a new route, and in 1979 he led a team of six to the top of the world's second-highest mountain, K2 (28,251 feet [8,611 m]). In 1983, he led a party on a notable ascent of Cho Oyu (26,906 feet [8,201 m]) using a new route, the southwest face. Messner was the first man ever to climb all fourteen of the world's mountains exceeding 8,000 meters (26,250 feet), and he was also the first to cross Antarctica without either dogs or machines.

Sir Edmund Hillary and Reinhold Messner

ABOUT THE AUTHOR

In 1980, Messner made the first solo ascent of Mount Everest (29,028 feet [8,848 m]), the world's highest peak, without the use of bottled oxygen. It was Messner's second ascent of Everest; his first climb in 1978 with Peter Habeler was the first ascent ever accomplished without additional oxygen.

Crossing Greenland on foot was Messner's most recent adventure.